© 1987 Frame House Gallery, Inc.

TERROR BY NIGHT

TERROR BY NIGHT

A Bomber Pilot's Story

Michael Renaut, DFC

WILLIAM KIMBER · LONDON

First published in 1982 by
WILLIAM KIMBER & CO. LIMITED
Godolphin House, 22a Queen Anne's Gate,
London, SW1H 9AE

Typeset by Robcroft Ltd. London WC1
Printed in Great Britain by
Garden City Press Limited
Pixmore Avenue, Letchworth, Hart

Contents

		Page
Foreword by Group Captain David Young, DSO, DFC, AFC		11
I	Initiation	15
II	Operational on Whitleys	36
III	Operational on Halifaxes	59
IV	Middle East	96
V	Halifax Conversion Unit	127
VI	Number 100 Group	146
VII	Peace	168
	Epilogue	181
	Index	187

List of Illustrations

Facing page

Michael Renaut, 1941   32
Wing Commander David Young   33
Inspecting Renaut's Halifax after operations   48
Found after a trip to Brest *Crown Copyright*   49
Pilot Officer Renaut with flight engineer and navigator   64
Michael Renaut with Bill Kofoed   65
Renaut with Tim Collins   80
Michael and Yvonne Renault's wedding   81
Wing Commander Renaut commanding 171 Squadron   112
The improved Halifax   112
Hamburg from 18,000 feet   113
Cologne 1945   144
Another view of Cologne   145

Page

Government instructions for RAF personnel in the
    Middle East   101

To
Yvonne, John and Dr B
— my counsellors

Acknowledgements

I would like to thank Jeanette and Barney Hallam for the interest they have shown and the help they have given in preparing Michael's book for publication.

YVONNE RENAUT

Foreword

by

Group Captain David Young, DSO, DFC, AFC

Michael Renaut was one of the bravest men that I have known, and I have known many brave men.

Born in 1920 of middle class parents, he had a normal education, and after leaving school, he went to work for J. Lyons and Co. He was bright and cheerful, and had a great sense of humour and a vivid imagination. I am convinced that in the end it was the imagination that killed him.

Bravery is difficult to define and can be shown by a brainless 'tough guy' who sees something to be done, and does it because that is what he is trained to do. It can also be more subtle and prolonged. My admiration for both has no limits, and this book illustrates the constant anxiety and fear under which bomber crews worked, not only for the long hours over enemy territory, but the even longer hours before take-off, from first thing in the morning until they were back safely on the ground after perhaps eighteen hours from the time that the crews' names were on the board.

The underlying anxiety coupled with real fear drained away courage which has been so well described as an expendable asset. That is why the authorities in their wisdom decreed that thirty night operations against the enemy was enough for one tour. After that there was a compulsory 'rest' from operations in a training school. It was a good sound average, but the trouble is that few people are average. For that matter, very few crews survived the full thirty operations. There were those who could do a full tour and ask for more, and if they were good enough, they could go to Pathfinders.

But there were those who could not stand the full thirty, and their squadron commanders had great difficulty in deciding what to do with them. Five or six trips and a fellow packs up; the answer is easy to reach and hard to carry out. The boy was posted LMF, meaning Lacks Moral Fibre which was a euphemism for cowardice and was treated severely.

In fact no one in the early days of the war understood that a man's nerve could shatter to the extent that he was quite incapable of continuing to work accurately in the face of his fear.

All aircrew were volunteers for the work and if one or two in a hundred found that they had 'not got what it takes' after a few operations, it was necessary that they be got out of sight at once and in ignominy in case they contaminated others. They could be terribly bad for the morale of the squadron.

All men are not created equal whatever Jefferson may have said. Some can run a mile or more, and some cannot run a hundred yards. Some can learn several languages, and others have difficulty in speaking their own. In just the same way some men could control their fears and others could not.

So although LMF cases had to be got rid of at once because they did not come up to the high standard required, it must be remembered that they had in the first place volunteered for what was probably the most dangerous branch of the armed services, and are not to be classed with plenty of young and fit men who persuaded themselves and others that they must stay in some reserved occupation throughout the war.

But what of the man who does twenty-eight, twenty-five or twenty operations and cannot take any more? The MO supports him and wants to take him off flying. Some clerk in a nice safe office knows the rules and says, 'He failed to complete his contract so he is LMF.' The squadron commander then has a battle on his hands to protect a gallant young man who has done his best, but who was not a 'tough guy'. I only remember having to deal with this situation twice but I am sure other CO's had it, and I do remember how furious I was with the junior officer who had never done any flying himself and yet presumed to sit in judgement.

However, this is about Michael Renaut and he was never suspected of failing. He was an above average pilot, but highly strung. More so as time went on, but he never wavered. Time after time he came back with photographs of his aiming point and an aircraft damaged by flak. A lot of credit goes to his navigator, Tim Collins. They were a very sound and successful team, and I think that Tim who was a few years older was a steadying influence on Michael's emotions. This book illustrates how courageous Michael was. Time after time he tells how frightened he was, but never a word of how he pressed on in spite of it.

Many books have been written about war experiences. Some are autobiographical, some are fiction, but I have never seen one written as this one, with the accent on fear, a man's own fear. Michael is quite candid and there is no attempt to glamourise himself, quite the reverse. Nor does it contain any fiction. It was necessary for everyone to ignore fear, and pretend that it did not exist, and he was naive enough to think that this was just his guilty secret, and no one else could experience that sinking emotion. He even wrote to me in 1962 and asked me to tell him candidly if I had ever experienced fear, and under what circumstances!

So, after the war he went back to his very kind civilian employers. He had no difficulty about being unemployed as were so many men, but his courage under fire for so long had sapped his strength, and he was constantly afraid when there was no longer reason to fear. He feared that he might get the sack for inefficiency, but he was not inefficient. Eventually he left that safe job because he was persuaded to go and work at selling motor cars, where he thought he had better prospects. Again he was successful but when he was given more responsibility it broke him, and he had a nervous breakdown. He recovered after treatment but a few months later had another breakdown. He died on 31st January 1964.

I do not know what was on the death certificate, but I know what I would have written: 'This man gave the whole of his abundant courage to his Country during six years of war. There was nothing left.'

Among those who attended his funeral service in the crowded church were his ex-Station Commander and his ex-AOC Air Marshal Sir Roderick Carr, both of whom had known and admired him and still remembered him after twenty years.

CHAPTER ONE

Initiation

I always wanted to fly – right from the days when, as a child my mother took me to air displays and for five shillings you could have a flight with Sir Alan Cobham. I was eight when I had my first flight at Herne Bay – just three miles along the coast to Reculver and back to the field, and I loved it. Later my mother took a picnic lunch and we went to Croydon to watch the aeroplanes take off and land (Imperial Airways 'Hannibals').

One afternoon I booked a ten shillings 'aerobatics' flight in a DH Puss Moth and waited anxiously by the aeroplane for the pilot to emerge from his office. When he came out he was dressed in sports coat and flannels and carried a helmet – I was so disillusioned; I'd imagined a 'superman' clad in flying suit and goggles! Aerobatics were thrilling and I was one of the lucky ones who never felt airsick. So one August morning in 1940, on the spur of the moment, I walked into an RAF recruiting station in Acton and said to the sergeant in charge, 'I want to join the RAF.' To which he replied, 'I suppose you want to be a pilot – they all do.' I admitted it and he asked me how my trigonometry was. A bit taken aback I had to own up that it was awful. The sergeant said, 'The best thing you can do is to buy a book on trigonometry and start swotting it up; we'll consider your application in due course.'

So I went straight to the nearest Smith's bookstall and bought a book on trig and took it to work with me so that I could start re-learning it. However, when I got home that same evening (such was the postal service in those days!) there was a postcard waiting for me, requesting me to attend a medical examination at the Air Ministry at 9.30 the next morning.

There followed the most comprehensive medical examination imaginable – eyesight, hearing, breathing, blood pressure, heart, throat, muscles, reflexes – in fact, a complete and thorough check-

up on every part of one's body. The following day came an
intelligence test, which turned out to be in two parts, one written
and the other oral. The written was fairly straightforward, but the
oral was held in front of five elderly and senior RAF officers, who
looked and sounded most forbidding. The sergeant had tipped me
in the waiting room not to guess at the answers; if one didn't know, it
was best to say, 'I don't know, sir.'

I was asked the teaser about the black and white socks in a drawer
in a darkened room – what was the minimum number of socks that
one needed to bring out of the darkness to ensure that one had two
of the same colour? My correct answer of 'Three' gave me a little
confidence for the next question. I was then asked whether, given a
stick, a ball of string, and a ruler, I could mark out a tennis court and
how I would do it. This was all right too, but I was floored by the
third question: 'If it is 3.00 p.m. in London, what time is it in New
York?' I promptly said, 'I don't know, sir' but the examiner insisted
and kept on saying, 'Come, come; you must know.' It was no good,
but luckily it didn't seem to matter, as after a wait outside while
presumably my fate was discussed, the Chairman of the Selection
Board said; 'Renaut, you have been selected as a pupil pilot/
navigator – good luck!'

I was still gaily under the impression that all this was just a
necessary preliminary to joining the Air Force, and that there was
no urgency about being called up and I next went through the
ceremony of attestation thinking that in about three months' time I
might hear something. I was soon disillusioned; 'AC2 Renaut,' said
the sergeant in charge, 'Your RAF number is 1375043 and you will
report to Babbacombe No 1 Receiving Wing tonight!!'

I was almost too flabbergasted to speak, and when I recovered I
asked if I could possibly have a week's leave to pack my things and
break the news to my parents and to my employers. This appeared
to be an outrageous request and the sergeant warned me that it
might prejudice my chances of a commission, but after a lot of
argument and pleading, I was grudgingly given forty-eight hours
leave.   . .

I now began to worry about what I had done, and also that I had
given false answers about my health on the form I had filled in. To
the question, 'Have you ever suffered from asthma, bronchitis and

hayfever?' I had answered, 'No', but I had had chronic attacks of asthma and hayfever from the age of four. I began to have fears about physical training as I couldn't run a hundred yards without striving for breath – in tests carried out on me at St Mary's Hospital Paddington, a year before, it was established that Michaelmas daisies, horses, hay and laughter brought on an attack.

My first move was to tell my parents what I had done; they were living at Bucklebury Common to avoid the air raids, so I journeyed down to see them. My mother was alarmed and apprehensive at my wanting to become a pilot, but I soothed her by telling her that I'd be safe for at least a year because of the training period. My employers, J. Lyons & Co., were very nice about my enlistment; my Director, Sam Salmon (now Sir Samuel Salmon), told me that I could easily have got a commission in the Army Catering Corps if I'd so wished, but I was determined to make my own way as Aircraftman Second Class Renaut!

I reported to No 1 Receiving Wing at Babbacombe on 12th August feeling not unlike a fledgeling grouse, in view of the date, and was kitted out in ill-fitting RAF uniform and informed in no uncertain terms that I needed a haircut. Not wishing to incur the wrath of the parade sergeant, I dropped everything and went to have one. However, I had yet to learn that a service haircut was different from *my* idea of a haircut, and the sergeant produced the old chestnut on parade; standing behind me, he shouted: 'Am I hurting you?' – 'No, Sergeant.' – 'Well I ought to be, 'cos I'm standing on your 'air.' To my dismay it took something akin to a crewcut to satisfy him.

Life became an endless round of parades and drill, but the war still seemed far away until one morning, when we were all on parade on Babbacombe Downs, a German Heinkel bomber swooped down on us and sprayed machine-gun bullets. The command 'Scatter' rang out and Renaut was one of the first to dive for cover, but the aircraft was by then on its way inland and we could clearly see bombs fall on what we later learned was Newton Abbot railway station. There were two full trains in the station at the time and the death roll was very high. We later saw the Heinkel make for home across the Channel hotly pursued by a Hawker Hurricane which shot it down some five miles out to sea. I remember cheering like mad, in common with everyone else.

The Receiving Wing was under the command of Wing Commander Angiers and lectures were held in the local theatre which had been commandeered by the RAF. The most amusing lecture was given by the unit medical officer, who warned us that, 'Cupid shoots his arrow after the chemists shops are shut,' and 'Six months ago I couldn't pass a public house, but now I can pass broken bottles!' His warning of the dangers of VD could hardly be taken seriously!

Nineteen-forty was a lovely summer and I look back with pleasure at the fun we had, eating good food, attending lectures, hitting the high spots in Torquay with scores of new-found friends, going to bed early and feeling fit. There was one occasion when early in the morning I awoke to the scream of falling bombs and was out of, and under my bed in three seconds flat; the bombs fell a hundred yards from our billet and blew in our windows. One of two of the stick of bombs were delayed action and one had apparently buried itself in a garage adjoining a house on the cliff edge; we waited and watched most of the following day until that evening the bomb exploded and most of the house and garage went down the cliff.

After three weeks at Babbacombe, we were all paraded in the theatre to hear our future and my name was luckily included in the first fifty who were to go to No 3 Initial Training Wing at Torquay under the command of Air Commodore Critchley; others less fortunate were posted to Aberystwyth and beyond, but for me it just meant moving two or three miles along the coast.

We were billeted in the Regina Hotel in Torquay and our life consisted of physical training, lectures on armaments, air navigation, aircraft recognition, morse code, semaphore, meteorology and mathematics (but *no* trigonometry, which shows how wrong recruiting sergeants can be!). It was here that I learned the rudiments of the internal combustion engine – 'induction, compression, expansion, exhaust' – but I was never much of an engineer and a good deal of it was above my head. Luckily I shone at morse and mathematics, nor did I mind the drill. The PT got me down, as it meant running up the hill to Torquay downs and my asthma was vile but somehow I managed to conceal it from my superiors.

Ralph Pett-Frazer was a friend of mine and he used to come to Torquay and take me out; we used to go to the local theatre where we each had a girl friend – mine was Cynthia Rawson, a singer, who later married Tommy Fields, Gracie Fields' brother. Unfortunately the nicer hotels like the Imperial and the Queens were out of bounds to other ranks, but despite this there was plenty to do and no shortage of girls, as the Prudential Assurance Company had moved to Torquay from London and we shared the same air-raid shelters. There was something rather nice about sitting in a dark air-raid shelter with a 'Pru' girl on one's knee, and night raids were pretty frequent.

It was, of course, a strict rule that one had to be in by midnight (or 23.59 in service parlance) and one night Oakes, Selby Lowndes and I returned to our billet at about 1.00 a.m. only to find that the entrance road alongside the harbour was guarded with barbed wire and a sentry with fixed bayonet. After a hurried conference in the darkness we decided that the sentry would have to be pushed into the harbour and accordingly, as soon as we were challenged and before we were identified, the sentry was sent on his way, rifle and all! I have often wondered who the poor man was as I should like to apologise for our action, but at the time it was him or us! (Luckily the water was warm in September and very shallow, so he survived.)

After six weeks of intensive training under the command of Flying Officer L.E.G. Ames (the well-known England and Kent cricketer) we were all fit and bursting with knowledge and once again we attended a parade to hear our next move. We had done several 'aptitude tests' like pushing shaped pieces of wood into a square and round holes, but evidently this was to establish whether we were to be bomber or fighter pilots, though how this was done God above knows.

We were all (fifty of us) posted to Marshalls Flying School at Cambridge for initial training and there followed five weeks of really intensive training; flying in the morning and ground studies in the afternoon and then vice versa.

It was on 20th October 1940 that I had my first flight in a Tiger Moth, with an instructor named Pilot Officer Mallorie. Never shall I forget the thrill of it – of becoming airborne and looking down on the jigsaw of fields, roads and houses. This, of course, was an open seat plane, very noisy and very windy and quite unlike anything that flies today. I loved the Tiger Moth dearly, but Mallorie had a very sarcastic streak and a caustic sense of humour. His favourite expression was, 'Renaut, don't fly it like a horse and cart' and 'Be more gentle with my aeroplane, if you please.'

My other instructors were Sergeant Tappin and Sergeant Sparrow, who were both charming, but I was terribly bad at flying Tiger Moths and the hours of dual instruction began to build up. Generally speaking, one soloed at between eight and ten hours dual instruction, but Renaut was so incompetent that he looked like being failed as a pilot.

I remember one morning having take-offs and landings with Mallorie and when I came in for a time-check the clerk said, 'Forty minutes'.

The time had gone so quickly I couldn't believe it, so I went up to Mallorie and said, 'Sir, that flight didn't seem like forty minutes to you, did it?'

'Renaut,' he replied, 'It seemed like forty years!'

I was anxious to keep down my hours of dual instruction.

I simply couldn't master landings and my dual instruction had reached fourteen and a half hours, so I was due for a CFI (Chief Flying Instructor) test next day, failure in which automatically meant rejection as a pilot. Mallorie had never told me where to look when holding off to land. The correct way was to cock one's head to one side and look ahead down towards the nose but through ignorance I was looking straight ahead through the air screw and naturally I couldn't see a thing beyond the nose. Had I been taught the right way, looking back, I feel I could have soloed so much earlier. Sergeant Tappin gave me a further forty minutes dual instruction and I begged him to let me fly solo but he was very doubtful and most reluctant to let me try. Anyway I pleaded with him and eventually he climbed out of his seat, wished me luck and said, 'For heaven's sake, don't break it.'

So off I went, that afternoon of 8th November, flying solo at last and I was so excited and elated that over the aerodrome at a thousand feet, in sheer joy I quite forgot the approach to land. I then saw Tappin sitting disconsolately at the edge of the field and I suddenly realised that I must put the aircraft down gently and in one piece, which I did. So after all, there was no CFI test for me the next day. This of course was only the beginning, and several hurdles lay ahead in the form of aerobatics, air navigation, steep turns, gliding, stalling and spinning.

One day we all witnessed an amusing incident. We had been taught how to swing the airscrew to start the engine – a tricky business as one had to back smartly away when the engine fired and then climb in the cockpit and taxi away. Neville Tree was swinging the airscrew of his Tiger Moth when the engine sprang into life and he had evidently left the throttle partly open, for the Moth started to move away before he had time to hop in the cockpit. All he managed to do was to grasp hold of the port wing tip whilst he and the Moth orbited round on the ground with Neville shouting for help!

I was lucky enough to be billeted on the Chivers jam family in Cambridge, but I never met my host and hostess – I was always up at 6.30 a.m. and back too late at night, but they always left me a trolley of drinks and the maid looked after me. There was plenty to do in Cambridge and we frequently went to the Arts Theatre and restaurant where we fed like fighting cocks. Our bunch seemed always to include Richard Oakes, Neville Tree, Geoff Thomas and John Pershke, and Richard and Geoff became my closest friends. The strain was beginning to tell although we didn't really know it, and we became like schoolboys on the verge of taking matriculation – that sort of fear that we would fail the written yet pass the practical – one of many fears that were to crowd in as the years went on.

My second solo flight was to practise spinning and looping the loop and Tappin warned me that it was very important not to get lost. He advised me to fly to a landmark like a factory chimney and then climb up to eight thousand feet and, after spinning down, find the chimney again and repeat the process. Off I went flying like a dog with two tails at the thought of a solo flying; I located a nice big chimney, climbed up to eight thousand feet as I had been told and did my first solo spin. All one did was to hold the nose of the Moth upwards until one's speed fell to about 45 mph and then kick the rudder hard to right or left and the Moth's nose would fall and spin.

The sensation was marvellous; the jigsaw of the earth below rotated and one might spin ten or twenty times before pulling out at about three thousand feet. The cure for a spin was simply to put the nose hard down and apply full opposite rudder to the direction of the spin whereupon one would fly normally again. Once again I climbed to the same height and tried a couple of loops and then spun down once more to three thousand feet, only this time my factory chimney was miles away to the right; I was quite surprised at the distance but I put it down to inexperience and inaccurate loops.

I eventually reached my chimney and started to climb for a final spin and after this was completed I hastily flew to it again only to realise that it was not the same one!! There lay the temptation to panic for by now it was raining hard and the clouds were low, but I tried to remember all I'd been taught about forced landing. I simply hadn't any idea where I was and I was very frightened of either running out of petrol or crashing – and scared at being lost. I searched in wide circles for some washing on a line so that I could tell the wind direction (as we had been taught to do) but it was evidently not a Monday and no-one had any out, so I tried to find a house with a smoking fire but nobody even had one in the grate, and I had to resort to a passing steam train, which wasn't the easiest form of wind identification! I then selected a nice big field and flew over it to examine the surface which was pockmarked with bomb craters. However, it was a huge field and I was reasonably confident that I could find a smooth stretch and enough length to land a Tiger Moth, which required a very little yardage.

I made my approach to land into the wind as far as I could tell but the moment I started to hold off I realised that I was travelling crabwise across the field; but it was too late to do anything and I held my breath and made an atrocious but damage-free landing.

I left the Tiger Moth and walked across to the building where I discovered that I had landed on Newmarket racecourse! There was a Wellington bomber squadron based there and I was fêted royally and allowed to attend an operational briefing as well as being given a meal. It was all very exciting and I felt like a schoolboy at an Old Boys' Reunion. They telephoned Cambridge and told Tappin where I was and he drove over in his car and brought two gallons of petrol in a can and then we flew back. Looking back, I think that my having forced landed on my second solo gave the CFI a good impression, and they probably had more faith in my ability to fly than I had at the moment.

It was about this time that I suddenly realised that I hadn't had an attack of asthma since I first flew at Cambridge and yet I had been near horses, and I had certainly laughed a great deal, and strange to say, I have never had asthma since.

The aerodrome defence was somewhat erratic; there were a few Bofors guns scattered about in the hands of inexperienced gunners, but there was also a long line of rockets with wires attached which, when fired simultaneously in the face of an oncoming aeroplane, acted like a wire screen. I was fortunate enough to see this in operation one November morning when a Messerschmitt 109 beat up the aerodrome, only to find that his airscrew was suddenly shattered by the cables and the Hun promptly landed on his belly, furious and very bewildered.

We were a very happy course and my friendship with Richard Oakes flourished. He was a Christian Scientist and strange in many ways, but I liked him as much as he apparently liked me. The same was true of Geoff Thomas, who came from Rugby – he and I were later to share a flat in Darlington. Richard was a good driver and a very efficient flier; he survived the war but, strange to say, has since had six serious crashes in aeroplanes, any one of which could have killed him. He had a charmed life but, as a result of plastic surgery, he now looks a quite different person from the one I knew in 1940.

I didn't fly again with Mallorie until 19th November, when he found my flying much improved. He remained sarcastic and I was never at ease in the Tiger Moth when I could see the back of Mallorie's head in the front cockpit! The pilot always sat in the rear cockpit and the instructor in front. Each had a set of linked controls and the pupil could only see the back of the instructor's head in flight, which perhaps was a good thing. We did some more 'circuits and bumps' that afternoon and on my second landing I held off too high and Mallorie promptly shouted 'I've got her' and I saw the throttle lever pushed hard open.

It was too late; the engine would not respond to full throttle suddenly and consequently we stalled and fell nose down from about twenty feet. The crash was not too severe but I recall being hurt by the pull of my safety straps and I banged my head hard on the front of the cockpit. Mallorie swore like a trooper and was evidently chiefly concerned with the state of the Tiger Moth; actually the only damage it sustained was a smashed airscrew, a buckled wing-tip, and damage to the engine cowlings.

The only other excitement during the five weeks' course was Jock MacLeod bailing out. Jock, a crazy Scot, was having instruction in aerobatics with the Flight Commander, Flight Lieutenant Richardson, when suddenly the controls of the Moth failed to respond and Richardson gave the order to abandon aircraft. Jock was somewhat alarmed at this for like most of us, he simply regarded his parachute as something to sit on and having to really use it came as something of a shock. Anyway, from an inverted position he dropped from the Moth some two thousand feet and landed beside the main road into Cambridge quite unharmed. It was typical of MacLeod's coolness that he bundled the opened parachute under his arm and hitch-hiked his way back to Cambridge aerodrome.

I continued to be very poor at aerobatics; I could loop the loop and spin quite expertly but my slow rolls and half rolls of the top of the loop were atrociously bad. I could fly inverted quite happily too, except that all the dust and rubbish from the floor of the cockpit streamed past one's face, but I could never really get used to looking upwards and seeing the ground and looking downwards and seeing the sky, and in addition, as Mallorie said, I was inclined to fly the thing like a horse and cart and not a delicate aircraft.

We next embarked upon a whole series of cross-country flights, first as pilot with navigator, then as navigator with pilot, and we learned the rudiments of map reading and simple air navigation. I was again lucky enough not to have a final test with the CFI because I am sure he would have failed me on aerobatics. (I dreaded the thought of this ordeal but it never came!) I had passed all the oral and practical examinations and we were finally passed out on 23rd November 1940. My name was on the list to go to Moosejaw, Saskatchewan in Canada, for advanced flying training and I was thrilled at the thought, but at the very last moment I was called in to the Commanding Officer and told that two brothers were badly wanting to be together in Canada and would I stand down. As things turned out, this probably saved my life since of the fifty pilots on our course trained in Moosejaw only one was to survive the war.

The remainder of us were posted to No 11 Senior Flying Training Station at Shawbury, near Shrewsbury. This was an extremely pleasant station, designed and built on Cranwell lines – the food was excellent, the pupils' quarters warm and comfortable and the countryside beautiful. The course was to last twelve weeks but, knowing the English weather and Bob Hope's famous remark that 'only in England do you get all the four seasons in one day', we doubted whether the course could run to schedule. It didn't.

Our aircraft were twin-engined Airspeed Oxfords – pleasant aircraft to fly but possessing certain vicious characteristics with which we soon became familiar. They seemed large planes after the Tiger Moths and it was strange operating two throttles instead of one. I soloed after six hours dual instruction in them and began to feel quite confident at the controls – much more so than in the Tiger Moth.

But fear now began to creep into my thoughts again: fear that I was being drawn inexorably nearer to flying against Germany. It was a strange feeling because, although I was enjoying myself enormously, and had so many new and close friends, deep down in the pit of my stomach was this eerie feeling that with every hour I was coming nearer to possible death. If one refers to a dictionary, 'Fear' is explained as: 'A painful emotion, excited by danger.' This was just it as far as I was concerned; I realised the dangers of flying but these did not bother me as I felt that flying training was reasonably danger-free. It was the culmination I feared – the end of flying training and the beginning of bombing raids, and suddenly every hour of training became more precious; as precious to me as my life.

I never discussed my fears with anyone, not even Richard Oakes or Geoff Thomas, but in every moment of inactivity they came to the fore. I used to lie awake at night thinking of my father and mother and the strain I was about to put them through, and the fear of being posted as 'Missing, believed killed'. I read the papers daily and there among the headlines was 'Bomber Command last night attacked Essen and caused heavy damage. Twenty-one of our aircraft failed to return.' Twenty-one aircraft. That meant about one hundred and fifty men posted as missing; a few would be safe in enemy hands, but the majority would be burned to death, their bodies shattered by crashing or plunging into the sea. There was no dispelling this fear – it was there all the time, but depending on how busy you were, it either came to the fore or lurked below the surface. I longed to ask my friends if they felt as I did but I hadn't the kind of courage needed to do this and so the vital question remained unanswered.

Looking back, I had had fear since childhood – I was sent as a boarder to a preparatory school in Herne Bay when I was nine years old and I remember crying to myself in bed at the thought of my father and mother having rows – they were squabbles rather than rows but the fact remained that they made an impression on my mind. It was the same sort of fear with exams, and even when I'd left school and started work with Hall Crown Ltd, under Anthony Salmon, in Oxford Street, (owned by J. Lyons & Co Ltd) I lived in fear of losing my job because they were an efficient company and had no time for incompetence. It was really a matter of self-confidence, but I was too young to possess this quality to any extent.

On 9th December 1940 at Shawbury I had my first meeting with death. A young pupil was approaching to land when he must have allowed his airspeed to fall too low and he spun into the ground from five hundred feet. Incredibly the Oxford didn't burn, but I walked over to examine the wreckage on the edge of the airfield and stood in awe at the twisted, torn hulk of the aircraft. The body, shattered, had just been removed but there was a great deal of blood about and I was momentarily sickened imagining I was looking at the pilot in his seat, torn and dismembered.

I thought of the parents, and later, at the funeral, we slow marched to the cemetery and I dwelt upon the sadness this death had caused, the red-rimmed eyes of the mother and the comforting bereaved father hand-in-hand with her at the graveside. I suppose most of us were affected but no one showed any emotion at the time, and the accident was soon forgotten in the activity of the training school.

I remember the day after Coventry was blitzed Richard and I went sent off in an Oxford to do map reading and I suddenly said to Richard, 'Why not let's go and have a look at Coventry; it's not far?'

Richard agreed so I turned the nose towards Coventry and we were soon above the shattered city, staggered at the damage wrought by the Hun. Down I went to 300 feet (strictly against the rules!) to get a closer look at the rubble and empty shells of the houses when suddenly I saw a barrage balloon above me! We had both overlooked the balloon barrage and there we were, literally caught in a wire net! I thought as quickly as I could and opened up the throttles to full power and banked steeply to the left hoping that the aircraft literally standing on its wingtips would offer less of a frontage to the cables than if we flew straight and level. We were incredibly lucky and flew out of the barrage unscathed but both Richard's and my heart were beating madly and I have rarely been so frightened as I was at that moment.

They were happy days at Shawbury and our leisure hours were being spent on the top of Wrekin with its wonderful view, walking into Shrewsbury, going to cinemas, eating good food and devoting all our energies at work to the many subjects that constituted the 'Wings Exam'. It was almost like being at school with the impending exams. I was learning formation flying, cross-country flying, flying on one engine, stalling, landing without flaps, restarting engines in flight, and I was just beginning to become competent and to gain a fair degree of self-confidence. This applied particularly to instrument flying, which occupied a large part of our training. One had to learn to fly by instruments only and to have absolute confidence in those instrument readings even if they were contrary to the aircraft's attitude as one sensed it.

This was all necessary training for the night flying which loomed ahead, but constant delays beset us. Frequently we would be ready for night dual when the Hun would attack Liverpool and that meant a strict black-out and the flare-path being extinguished, so we would sit chatting and waiting for the all-clear, but it always came too late for us to embark on flying instruction.

Christmas 1940 brought the snow – just inches of it to begin with but transport in any form became impossible. Richard and I decided to walk eight miles into Shrewsbury in thick snow and we did it in two hours exactly, on Christmas Day. We went to the Red Lion where they held a special dinner and silly games afterwards. It was great fun and we enjoyed ourselves into the small hours but we certainly took longer than two hours to walk back! On 16th January 1941 the snow really fell, and there were drifts of up to fifteen feet on the aerodrome approach roads.

The Senior Administrative Officer ordered every man on the station to start digging a way to the village for supplies and we started in earnest on 17th January. After three days we had progressed about half a mile but we were all intensely irritated that the SAO had not set an example by volunteering to dig with us and accordingly we decided to set a trap for him. We knew that he and the Station Adjutant would inspect the progress daily so we dug an enormous cave under the hard trodden snow and left the usual path along by the telegraph poles so that when anyone stepped on to that section they would fall about eight feet into soft snow. The trap completed we waited anxiously for the inspection which we knew would be around 3.00 p.m. and sure enough we saw the SAO and the Adjutant approaching but sad to say, the Adjutant preceded his superior and disappeared in a flurry of snow three feet in front of the SAO! There was a great deal of laughter but none from the SAO who by now knew that the trap was set for him!

The arduous digging continued and it became bitterly cold that January. Richard and I were sharing a small RAF house on the aerodrome and we were determined to be warm and comfortable, so, strictly against regulations, Richard bought a twin element electric fire for our bedroom and gave me the job of wiring it up to the plug. This was my first attempt at electrical work; I knew insulation came into it somewhere, so to be on the safe side I bound the three wires together with insulating tape and eventually switched on; there followed a minor explosion and the entire station was plunged into darkness to the accompaniment of shouts and screams for light. Have you ever tried looking for a fuse-box in pitch darkness in snow on the outside wall of a house without a ladder? It wasn't easy but I eventually found the fuse-boxes and replaced the burnt-out fuse, having learnt the hard way that the place for insulation was between positive, negative and earth!

The snow stayed with us until 23rd February and we spent five weeks indoors swotting up for the exams, unable to take to the air once. By now we were all competent at morse, semaphore, meteorology, Link trainer, armaments, air navigation, aircraft recognition and the internal combustion engine – how we used to chant 'induction, compression, expansion, exhaust' until we were heartily sick of it!

I seemed to take to night flying like a duck to water and after only 1½ hours dual instruction by night I was sent solo. Never shall I forget that flight. I took off normally and commenced my circuit, then I got on the tail of another Oxford and joined circuit with him. But I got confused with the green Aldis lamp shown from the ground and wondered whether it was meant for him or me. Moreover, the other aircraft seemed to have a fatal fascination, and try as I would I couldn't shake it off. I found myself diving steeply to the left at 200 mph and my height was down to 100 feet and I only just missed the roof of a hangar. I just pulled out in time and started to regain height, absolutely scared stiff. Looking back, 1½ hours night instruction was obviously not enough and I was far from safe in an Oxford.

This numbing experience preyed on my mind afterwards with the realisation that I had been within a few feet of death. It took me some minutes to pull myself together, but at last I got back on the circuit and carried out my landing drill and finally put the Oxford down gently and in one piece. To my surprise I had been airborne for forty minutes and I told my instructor, Sergeant Sewell, how petrified I'd been and he very wisely gave me another forty minutes dual instruction on a dark night before sending me solo again.

By this time I was an LAC (Leading Aircraftman) and my pay was about 15/-d a week and with this, and what I was given by my parents I was able to live very comfortably. (My employers allowed my mother £1 per week all the time I was in the services – a very generous and kindly thing to do.) The thaw had set in now and Shrewsbury became flooded and we were given some leave so Richard and I set off in his Wolseley 16 hp to drive to London. This was a hazardous business because there were no signposts and we were driving behind hooded headlamps with a range of about 100 yards. I was map-reading and got us lost several times – the country seemed to swarm with culs-de-sac – but we did reach London. Funny to think that I could fly aeroplanes but couldn't drive a car – but this was to be remedied soon.

My parents were pleased to see me and I was showed off to all our relatives and friends. My uniform fitted me like a sack of potatoes but it represented a branch of the fighting services which was getting the whole of the press publicity and I felt proud to be a member of the RAF Volunteer Reserve – there on my lapels were the minute VR's to confirm it. I had to do a round of visits to all my relations and despite the strict security, I was recounting my experiences in detail since I felt that Hun spies would not benefit very greatly from this information.

On return from leave we resumed flying and quickly got back into the routine. Cross-country flights and formation flying were the order of the day and we began to fly further afield from the west. On 31st March I acted as navigator on a cross-country Shawbury-Scampton-Desford-Shawbury, and later on 6th April I piloted my Oxford on the same route. It was about this time that we saw a pupil nearly kill himself. He took off towards the hills and failed to lock the throttles with the result that they eased back after take-off and he lost power and very nearly crashed on the hillside. Luckily he must have tumbled to his error at the last second, for, breathlessly we watched the Oxford suddenly begin to gain height, and continue on its way. This was an easy pitfall and many of us had done the same thing at some time, but the remedy was simply to turn the locking screw clockwise and prevent the twin throttles from creeping back.

We were now on the verge of the Wings exam. Our problem child was LAC Selby Lowndes. He was a charming fellow, only nineteen like me, but he had little brain. His step-brother, Dicky Lee, had achieved fame as a fighter pilot and he was anxious to uphold the family tradition himself as poor Dicky Lee had been killed in the Battle of Britain. He had last been seen chasing nine Messerschmitt 109's back across the Channel to France and it is presumed that one or more of them turned back on him and shot him down. We were all desperately anxious to help poor Selby Lowndes at the Wings exam because it was perfectly obvious that on his own he would fail the written part.

The great day dawned and we were marched into this big classroom in the presence of an invigilator, to embark on the examination which was going to make or break us as pilots. Mathematics were anathema to Selby Lowndes but luckily they were my strong point and fate intervened in seating us alongside one another. I was thus able, under the eyes of the invigilator, 'accidentally' to drop my mathematics paper on the floor for Selby Lowndes to pick up. Yet somehow he only got the minimum pass of 60 per cent after copying my paper for which I was subsequently awarded 100 per cent!

Unbelievably, the lights fused during this exam and the whole room was plunged into darkness for about ten minutes and when the lights were restored not one pupil was in his seat! Meteorology was our weakest subject so we had an arrangement that at 5.00 p.m. the meteorological officer would be in the lavatory to answer questions. Miraculously the invigilator was not suspicious when several pupils in turn asked to be allowed to pass water. I went myself to verify some of my answers and the Met Officer was most helpful. He wanted us, as much as we did, to be successful.

The result came through in a day or two and everyone passed, including Selby Lowndes, and off we went in high spirits to buy the magic 'Wings' and sew them on our jackets. Looking back I sometimes wonder if we did the right thing in helping Selby Lowndes to pass, because two years later he killed himself and two other men. It appears that he was practising air-to-air firing with a drogue-towing aircraft when he collided with the towing aircraft and all three men were killed. Had we let things take their course all those men might still have been alive today.

At this stage of the war we were given a choice of career: bombers, fighters, Coastal Command, army co-operation etc., and John Pershke said it didn't matter a damn what one put down as they'd post us where they wanted anyway, so he asked for army co-operation (more or less as a joke) and they darned well agreed. Poor Pershke was most undone at the thought of flying Westland Lysanders with 'Pongos', but he was killed soon afterwards. Fate was strange and again it made one wonder whether he'd still be alive if he'd opted for another branch.

We were finally assembled in the main lecture room to hear whether we were to be officers or NCO's and I regretted bitterly the reason why I failed to get a commission. Since I was five years old I had had a habit of biting my fingers and this had not passed unnoticed by the SAO or the Station Commander. I now realised that my superiors had been watching me and undoubtedly this revolting habit had jeopardised my chances of being commissioned. Of my crowd, Richard, Pershke, Espley and Fair were commissioned, but Geoff Thomas, McLeod, Herbert, Corbisier, a charming Belgian boy, and I were promoted to sergeant pilots. I was only proud of one thing: my classification as an 'above average' Oxford pilot and this helped offset my disappointment.

Our postings came through and it meant saying goodbye to lots of friends, including Richard Oakes who was posted to a Coastal Command training school. Geoff Thomas and I were both posted to Kinloss in Northern Scotland to No 19 Operational Training Unit. I was told to report on 7th May. I caught a train to Glasgow and arrived at 9.30 on a Saturday night. Glasgow was incredible. Everyone appeared to be tight; everyone was singing in the streets, there were brawls on the pavement outside the pubs and I even saw a police constable going off duty with four bottles of beer in his pockets. I thought of Harry Lauder's famous 'When I've had a couple of drinks on a Saturday, Glasgow belongs to me.' I made my way to our billet – a boarding house somewhere in Glasgow – where I was greeted by a cheery – but sober – landlady who next morning gave me a breakfast I shall never forget: two fried eggs and five rashers of bacon, and she kept coming in and asking if I wanted more. This, after the one egg and two rashers a week in England.

Early next morning I boarded a train for Inverness and was deeply impressed by the beautiful scenery – the Spey Valley, Pitlochry, Boat of Garten, Grantown-on-Spey – it was all particularly wonderful to one who had never been further north than the Norfolk Broads. It was a very slow train and I arrived at Kinloss in the late afternoon. My first duty was to ring my mother as I'd promised her I would tell what aeroplanes I was to fly. Being frightfully security conscious I felt I couldn't tell her outright they were Whitleys. Instead, 'Think of where our furniture is stored,' I kept saying. This was Whiteleys, but it made no kind of sense to her. My dear mother was getting very confused and wanted to know what on earth furniture had to do with flying aircraft!

Kinloss turned out to be a Nissen hut affair and Geoff and I went along to look at a Whitley Mark IV. It seemed to us then a gigantic thing and we stood in awe under the colossal wings wondering how Whitleys ever took to the air.

Michael Renaut, 1941.

Wing Commander David Young (later Group Captain).

I soloed after 2½ hours dual instruction with Sergeant Scrivena as my second pilot and I found the aircraft to be gentle and viceless. One had to get accustomed to the size but apart from that it was not difficult to fly and I now had a total of one hundred and fourteen flying hours to my credit on all types. Single-engine landings were not easy and we received a good deal of instruction on this when carrying out circuits and bumps. I soloed at night after 2½ hours but this wasn't difficult as it never really got dark in June in Northern Scotland.

The aircraft we were now flying were clapped-out old Whitleys which had been put out to grass from the operational squadrons of Bomber Command. It is difficult to appreciate nowadays that one's airspeed was about 115 mph when there are aircraft today which cannot remain airborne at that speed! I felt like the pilots of the BE2c's in the 1914/18 war when they gazed upon the Halifaxes and Lancasters of the World War II.

This was only an eight weeks' course and we had quite a lot of time on our hands. On our days off Geoff and I motored south to Grantown-on-Spey, where there wasn't a Forces man to be seen. We stayed at the Strathspey Hotel, which was kept by a sweet couple who treated us like kings. They fed us royally, as well as providing us with shotguns and a rough shoot, fishing rods and a ghillie, petrol coupons for our car – in fact, anything to make our lives a pleasure. Furthermore they would not accept a penny from us, and we paid nothing for our stay in their hotel; such is the generosity of the Scots. It is undoubtedly true that hospitality increased the further one travels north in the British Isles – we certainly found it so. (This question was once put to the 'Brains Trust' who denied that it was a fact.)

Geoff and I were not great fishermen but we went off with a hamper, a boat and some fishing rods to Lochindor, a few miles from Grantown and there we spent a gloriously peaceful day just fishing quietly. There were plenty of fish about and we could see them rising, but we returned that evening with not a solitary fish between us and yet the following day in a competition on the same loch the winner landed 127 trout! Such was our prowess, and we came in for a deal of good-natured leg-pulling the next evening.

Geoff's car was a boon; it was only a small Standard tourer but it took us far afield. Our petrol ration was infinitesimal but we augmented the supply by milking Whitleys in the dead of night with rubber tubes and cans and we secreted our hoard on a country road five miles from the aerodrome under some bushes. 100 octane petrol was really too potent for our little car and it had to be diluted with paraffin, so Geoff very wisely had an auxiliary petrol tank fitted in the boot with a two-way tap. Thus we were able to start the engine on bought petrol and change over to the octane/paraffin mixture as soon as the engine became warm. One of the snags with our patent mixture was that quantities of blue smoke came out of the exhaust and it smelt horribly of paraffin; this was far worse when the engine was cold or had to stand idle for some time. One day Geoff and I were off to Grantown when we were suddenly stopped by two Scots policemen who stepped from behind some bushes. They questioned us about misuses of petrol, but not seriously, and then stopped chatting to us for about half an hour. Geoff and I were petrified that they would smell the paraffin. At long last they said goodbye and Geoff accelerated away, enveloping the two policemen with a dense cloud of paraffin smoke. I remember looking back and seeing those policemen with dilated nostrils but with the suggestion of a smile on their lips.

Neither Geoff nor I had any girl-friends and we spent all our free time shooting, fishing and Scottish dancing. Rough shooting was great sport and we used to come back to Strathspey Hotel with masses of hares, rabbits, pheasants and even plovers – but food was scarce, and eventually we caught twelve trout in the River Spey between us.

It was at Grantown that we learned the custom of Whisky and Chasers and I've never forgotten that ghillie supping beer and whisky alternately and remaining firmly on his feet while Geoff and I were gradually drunk under the table. When we finally said goodbye to that ghillie at the end of the course we spent all night in his hut drinking and talking over his exploits. He promised to meet us at midnight one night and teach us the art of salmon poaching but unfortunately he got so whistled in anticipation that we eventually had to carry him to his bed and we never learned his wonderful system, that had to do with a wooden board and a number of hooks.

It was at Kinloss that we learned about bombing. There was a bombing range inland where we used to bomb large white triangles from about 10,000 feet with 11½ pound practice smoke bombs. At first we were not very good and I felt for the local inhabitants but later on we improved and were dropping four 250 pound bombs and learning to photograph the results.

My fears remained dormant at Kinloss. I knew that we were soon to join operational bombing squadrons, but life at the time was so full and happy that war seemed miles away. One is never entirely at ease in a heavier-than-air machine and there was always that underlying fear that one might crash. I don't think at this stage that this was a very real fear but there was always the uneasiness which undoubtedly led one to be boisterous and unnatural in one's behaviour.

The course ended on 14th July and Geoff and I set off in the tourer to motor to London non-stop from Inverness. We hadn't gone very far when the car started spitting and coughing and finally conked out altogether. It turned out to be water in the petrol, and we kept on having to stop and clean the carburettor. Progress was very slow indeed; I was map-reading because I couldn't drive, so poor Geoff had the strain of driving without a break and the inevitable happened. He fell asleep near Scotch Corner, and we struck the kerb at about 50 miles an hour and buckled the wheel. We were lucky not to have somersaulted but as it happened outside an Army Depot we had plenty of assistance in changing the wheel.

We reached London after eighteen hours at the wheel and Geoff and I went our separate ways. I went home to Bucklebury for seven days' leave and slept non-stop for twenty hours. My parents had moved there from London; it was lovely country and very peaceful, away from the air-raids. I only half enjoyed this leave because within a week I was to be posted to an operational squadron and this could mean sudden death. On the other hand I was excited and anxious to get started on the job of bombing Germany and my curiosity was suddenly aroused. I bluffed my mother that we wouldn't start operations immediately, but that we had a lot more training to do and to this day I wonder whether she believed me. Bless her heart, she kept every one of my wartime letters, numbered in sequence and parcelled up year by year. As I wrote to her twice a week for six years, one can imagine the collection and the newspaper cuttings and photos.

CHAPTER TWO

Operational on Whitleys

On 18th July 1941 I was posted to number 78 Squadron Middleton St George, on the borders of County Durham and Yorkshire. I arrived at Darlington Station in the late afternoon and took a taxi to the aerodrome. I asked the taxi driver what 78 Squadron was like, and he consoled me greatly by telling me that they hadn't lost a crew for six whole weeks. (So much for security!)

When I arrived the squadron was airborne on its way back from bombing the *Scharnhorst* and the *Gneisenau*, the German battle-cruisers, which were in dock on the Atlantic seaboard. Only eleven aircraft returned out of sixteen, which came as rather a shock to me after the taxi driver's report. It was, of course, a daylight raid and the risks were infinitely greater as there was no fighter escort. Strangely enough most of the casualties were the result of flak and not fighter opposition. (Flak translated in Flieger Abwehr Kanone or literally 'aeroplane-bugger-off-cannon'. Flak took many forms; light flak was hosepiped cannon in large quantities, medium flak was 2-4 inch shells, and ended up as large, black shell bursts, leaving behind a cloud of dense black smoke.)

Middleton St George was a peacetime station with comfortable messes and quarters, and was virtually modelled on Cranwell. It was completed, I believe, in 1939.

I first flew on the squadron on 27th July with Pilot Officer Jock Calder (later to achieve fame on 617 Squadron) just to familiarise myself with the locality. There were several good landmarks like Durham Cathedral and the balloon barrage at Billingham (the ICI Chemicals factory) and the long straight railway line from Thirsk and Northallerton to Darlington. Number 76 Squadron were also stationed at Middleton St George, but they had Merlin-engined Halifaxes; they made the Whitleys look very old-fashioned.

The sergeants' mess was very comfortable and the food excellent but there always seemed to be an atmosphere of urgency about the place. Darlington was only four miles away and we nearly always went there for our entertainment, particularly to the Imperial Hotel and its good food.

No 78 Squadron was commanded by Wing Commander Sawyer and No 76 Squadron by Wing Commander 'Bull' Jarman. Each squadron was split into 'A' and 'B' flights and I was under the command of Squadron Leader Jock Mercer, a Scot, who was slight of build and somewhat shy, but a brilliant and capable pilot who taught me a lot. Tragically he was killed on the night of 1st November in operations against Kiel. He was shot down by a German night fighter over the North Sea and there were, of course, no survivors. Hitting the sea in an aircraft is really no different from hitting a concrete wall, though it was not impossible to land on the sea with the undercarriage retracted and float for an hour or two.

We continued our training at Middleton St George – formation flying, flying on one engine and homing on beacons. I didn't relish formation flying, because I knew it was training for daylight raids and these were highly dangerous.

August 6th 1941 was a day I shall never forget; nightfall was to see my first operation, as second pilot to Pilot Officer Lowry, an experienced pilot with some twenty trips to his credit. In the morning we tested the Whitley No Z6742 and the target was to be Frankfurt. All day I experienced a strange feeling inside me, not entirely fear, a feeling of apprehension and yet an excited antici- pation of real danger. This was the culmination of all our training; I had dreaded it and yet now I wanted it to happen and happen quickly. As the hour drew nearer for briefing I became mentally and physically calmer and at the briefing itself, when the target was announced I even began to look forward to it. The Meteorological Officer painted a poor picture of the weather over the Continent and it appeared that we were going to encounter a good deal of cloud.

Take-off was planned for midnight, so there was a long spell of time to kill. I played snooker indifferently as I had other things to think about. What would it be like? Would we be chased by night fighters? What would the flak be like over the enemy coast? Finally we had our 'last supper' of bacon and egg; this was always given to operational aircrew despite the egg shortage and one relished the treat.

After a long and weary cockpit drill we taxied on to the runway and became airborne about midnight, crossing the English coast at Flamborough Head. All was quiet save for the roar of the two synchronised engines as we climbed slowly to 14,000 feet and the occasional exchange of verbal checks over the radio telephone. 'Captain to rear gunner, OK?' 'All OK Skipper.' and so on through the crew of five. We began to suffer severe icing in the dense cumulus cloud and this affected our rate of climb. Lowry didn't seem concerned but I was somewhat alarmed by the noise of chunks of ice as they flew off the airscrew tips and banged against the side of the fuselage. We had all put on our oxygen masks at 10,000 feet and we looked like men from Mars with our flying helmets, masks and Sidcot suits.

'Captain to navigator: how long before we cross the enemy coast?' 'Navigator to Skipper: eight minutes.'

Eight minutes was an eternity but suddenly we could hear the noise of bursting shells all round us and we felt the shock as they came close. Statistics showed that a shell had to burst within about 20 feet of an aeroplane to bring it down so one realised that gunfire would have to be extremely accurate before it became lethal. Nevertheless it was unnerving being shot at in thick cloud and my mouth went dry with sheer fright. What was lethal was when several guns put up a box barrage on one's course and one had no option but to fly through it. We were soon out of range of the coastal batteries and all was quiet again.

'Captain to Navigator: ETA target?' (Estimated time of arrival). 'Navigator to Skipper: 0420 hours.'

We were now in the midst of a severe electrical storm at 14,000 feet, still icing and still in broken cumulus cloud, when suddenly there was an enormous bang and flash and all the lights went out.

'Captain to crew: prepare to bale out.'

We had been struck by lightning and the trailing wireless aerial had burned up to its fixing point between the wireless operator's legs. The W/O was frantic and quite thought he had done himself an injury, but all was well apart from the pilot's compass spinning and the engines running out of phase. I went a mass of goose-pimples and thought to myself, 'What a beginning, to bale out and be taken prisoner on my first trip!' I thought of the telegram to my parents; 'Regret to inform you your son, M.W. Renaut, missing, believed killed night of 6th August.'

Lowry took stock of the situation and made his decision to jettison the bombs inside the German border as we'd used an excessive amount of petrol climbing through icing conditions and had lost height considerably after being struck. Accordingly we jettisoned our bomb load over Germany, twenty miles east of Luxembourg and turned the nose for home. I sat and pondered what would happen when the bombs exploded; would they fall harmlessly in open fields or would they destroy a small, sleepy village beneath? There in the second pilot's seat I felt let down at having missed the excitement of bombing a specific target and I wondered how much flak we would have seen over Frankfurt, which was heavily defended.

Lowry had now regained control and decided to climb to 20,000 feet to avoid icing and get above the warm front. We recrossed the enemy coast and heard a few more desultory bangs and then began to lose height fairly quickly. We touched down at 0540 hours, long before the rest of the squadron, and went in for de-briefing and bacon and eggs. I felt cheated at not having achieved anything on my first trip but I was elated at having got back in one piece. The wireless operator's trousers were scorched but apart from that there were no casualties.

Two days later we were briefed for the docks at Kiel and again I was sent as second pilot to Lowry. Kiel was a popular target with the aircrews because it was nearly all sea crossing and very little time, comparatively, over enemy territory. This time the weather conditions were ideal, with a full, bright moon. We could see the barrage at Kiel from eight miles away and it looked formidable. Suddenly nine Messerschmitt 109's in vic formation passed about 250 yards in front of us. I prayed to God they hadn't seen us because it meant curtains for us if they attacked, but luckily we saw nothing more of them.

Sergeant Beardmore, one of our OTU course, had been to Kiel as a second pilot some nights before and he amused us in the sergeants' mess with his description of the flak. He was thrilled with it and kept on saying how 'pretty' the light flak was – 'lots of coloured balls coming up to you; just like the 4th of June at Eton.' Its killing power was something he overlooked! To him it was simply a pleasure to see!

Beardmore was a case. In peace-time he owned greyhounds and every day in the mess he had a stack of letters from his trainer. We used to pull his leg about it and kidded him that he knew nothing until one day we said, 'Let's go to Stockton dog track and see what you really know.'

He fell for this and four of us went in Geoff's car to Stockton for the first race at 2.30 p.m. We had to be back at 5.30 for briefing so there was just time to see the six races and no sooner than we walked in the place, Beardmore recognised an old friend. Beardmore was a cockney, and to hear these two talking a foreign language about greyhounds made me laugh; what with '6 to 4' and 'No 5 will piss it' and 'look at that bleedin' mongrel, hasn't got a cat's 'ell's chance' I felt in another world.

Beardmore bet in pounds from a great wad of notes in his battledress pocket but we simply followed his selections in shillings. In the end we backed all six winners and I came away with £18. Beardmore must have won about £100 but we were happy. We drove back to Middleton for briefing and we all planned to go to Stockton every meeting. We were going to make our fortunes at the dogs but Beardmore was killed that night flying second pilot to Sergeant Malet-Warden. Nothing was ever heard of the crew.

Kiel drew nearer and the flak barrage was like an inferno – they were obviously firing from ships and the shore batteries and one could see aircraft coned in the searchlights in front of us. We started our approach down Kieler Hafen, came under heavy fire and quite suddenly we were caught in a searchlight and then a dozen or more in quick succession. This was my first experience of searchlight and they were absolutely blinding; one felt so naked and the flak became intense at our height of 12,000 feet.

I could hear fragments of shell banging and cutting through the Whitley and I found myself lowering my head to try and escape danger. This was quite ludicrous as the thin metal fuselage offered no more protection than the Perspex window but somehow one felt safer and it was better not to look out at the flak. We were coned for twelve minutes and it seemed like an eternity as we made our bombing run across the docks. The town was burning and this cast some light on the docks. I could see it all quite clearly.

The navigator suddenly shouted, 'Bombs gone' and we felt the old Whitley shudder as she shed her load. Unfortunately most of our stick of bombs landed in Kiel harbour but with some of them we straddled the buildings and dock installations.

At this stage Bomber Command was not a very accurate weapon; in the event of cloud cover over or near a target the accuracy was pitiful. We had not got PFF (Pathfinder Force) under the command of Don Bennett nor had we the navigational aids like Gee and H2S – these were to come later. A maximum effort from Bomber Command meant a force of under 650, composed of Whitleys, Wellingtons (which bore the brunt) Halifaxes, Lancasters, Stirlings, Manchester and Hampdens, (the last two were suicidal). The Short Bros 'Stirling' had many fine qualities and was delightful to handle but it never succeeded as a bomber because its ceiling with a bomb load was pathetically low. I only discovered the reason when I spoke to their Chief Test Pilot after the war. This was because several feet had to be trimmed off the wingspan after the design of the prototype in order to get it into the standard RAF hangar! Thus a certain amount of necessary 'lift' was sacrificed because the Air Ministry would not (or could not) alter the hangar entrance width. How we ever won the war with such master planners I just do not know!

On a fine night in a not too heavily defended target the Command strike was reasonably effective and a good deal of damage was caused in the residental areas. The effect of this on the Hun was not really worth the losses, any more than their destruction of the City of London was of value of them. Later, of course, the accurate destruction of small, important targets was far more effective and we can count ourselves lucky that the enemy didn't pursue such a strategy over Britain.

We shook ourselves free of Kiel, and Lowry allowed me to take over for the long flight back across the North Sea. Once well clear of the enemy coast we lost height down to 2,000 feet, took off our oxygen masks and out came the thermos flasks. That hot cup of coffee was a livener and conversation over the radio telephone became voluble. It was like a reprieve from the death sentence and we all behaved like happy schoolboys.

My next trip was to Hanover with another PO as captain. He was an untidy and jittery pilot whose flying, at times, was appalling (he was killed later). This was on 14th August and the full moon was a godsend when it came to bombing, but a curse if one was attacked by night fighters. It was amazing how far one could see on a moonlit night at 15,000 feet – looking into the western horizon in May and June, long after the sun had set, it was possible to see other aircraft five to ten miles away, quite clearly. The night fighters had no need of radar or ground control guidance, they simply used their 'eyes'. Even on a pitch dark night, one soon became 'dark-accustomed' and I, for one, could often spot another aircraft 1,000 yards away. My eyesight was classified as 'exceptional' in my medical exam and it stood me in good stead.

It was only in 1942 and later that we had such aids as Gee and H2S. I well remember the security that surrounded the intro- duction of Gee and all our crews were assembled in the briefing room to learn of this new device which was compared in effect to the introduction of the tank in the 1918 war. I am not an expert on radar, but this instrument was a sinysle radar screen which gave one's exact position over land and one could bomb accurately through dense cloud, without ever seeing the ground target. H2S was an improvement on Gee in that the navigator could actually see a 'television picture' of the ground below. Towns, rivers and coastlines stood out boldly and we were thus able to bomb a target as far away as Berlin without once seeing the ground after take-off.

Unfortunately the Hun soon learned of the device through his intelligence and what he salvaged from crashed bombers, and was able to design a counter device which used H2S as a means of 'homing' on to bombers and after that we could only use it as far as the enemy coast. The 'television' set had an explosive device fitted so that anything more than a heavy landing destroyed it. Fighter Command had similar devices for homing on to German bombers by night; the newspapers plugged the publicity of our night fighter pilots eating raw carrots to improve their night vision whereas, in truth, this was a cover for the secret devices in use at the time. We were undoubtedly far ahead of the Germans in radar but they soon had their own radar network which was equally effective.

We encountered seven to ten-tenths cloud most of the way to the target and after the usual greeting at the Dutch coast we had no trouble with searchlights. The weather cleared perfectly some twenty miles from the target and we could see very heavy flak to the west of Hanover, but we were left alone. This, of course, was ominous and usually indicated that night fighters were about.

Sure enough, the rear gunner spotted a Junkers 88 on our tail, and only about 700 yards behind us. The fateful voice came over the R/T:

'Rear gunner to Captain. Fighter approaching 700 yards astern.'

My reaction was a dry mouth and goose pimples at the funereal voice of the rear gunner. I was quite sure this was the end. Any second now the Ju88 would open fire and we should hear and feel his cannon shells ripping into us – but I hadn't reckoned on Frandsen; he suddenly started taking violent avoiding action and treated the old Whitley like a Tiger Moth. He was literally flinging the aircraft all over the sky and presenting, of course, a very different target to the Hun, who soon cleared off in disgust.

We all breathed again. We bombed accurately in the perfectly clear sky; and we had the satisfaction of materially adding to the fires down below in Hanover. The return trip was uneventful save for the landing at the base which resembled an elephant sitting down! Frandsen's landings were well known but I was quite content to have survived my third trip and didn't take much part in the subsequent leg-pulling.

Geoff Thomas and I now decided to live out and we took two furnished rooms in Darlington. This was strictly against the regulations but who was to know that we weren't among the hundreds in the sergeants' mess? I did all the cooking while Geoff attending to the bedmaking and keeping the flat clean. It was great fun and we lived there for five months before I was given a commission.

I went again on operations with Frandsen on 16th August and this time the target was Cologne. However, at the Dutch coast at 10,000 feet the oxygen supply failed and Frandsen decided to return to base.

I noted the following in my diary:

At 10,000 feet over the Dutch coast oxygen supply failed so Captain decided to return. Terrifying landing made at approx 20 feet at 80 mph. Frandsen never saw flarepath and made four 'landings' on the grass alongside the runway eventually coming to a rest at a dispersal point. Total flying time 6 hrs 40 mins.

We suffered about a week's bad weather and my next trip as second pilot was not until 24th August with Pilot Officer Calder (later to gain great distinction in the Dam Buster Squadron). At briefing the target was announced as Düsseldorf and my heart sank to my boots at the thought of the dreaded Ruhr – here was the biggest concentration of flak and searchlights in the whole of Germany and most crews felt the same way. Berlin was bad enough but the Ruhr was universally hated as a target.

We took off in ideal meteorological conditions and crossed the coast at Dunkerque where we endured very heavy and accurate flak. Calder was at 9,000 feet and after ten minutes' severe flak he decided to fire the enemy cartridge from the Very pistol. It said something for the British Intelligence service that each night before ops we were told the German cartridge colours for that night. These might be two reds and a green or yellow and white and were used in strict emergencies only (like sending out an SOS). I have known it to happen that we had been on the runway, about to take off, when the duty flying control officer would run to the fuselage door announcing a change of colours. This meant a rapid last minute change of cartridges, but some unknown British agent had risked his life and obtained the latest enemy colour combination and transmitted the information to Britain. With counter intelligence the Hun mostly knew our colours too!

We duly fired the cartridge and the effect was startling – all the flak died away and the searchlights switched off!! It was only a short run from Dunkerque to the Ruhr and we soon saw the battery of eight hundred searchlights and several times more flak batteries. I remember this trip vividly because it was the first time I saw an aircraft shot down at night. It was eerie to watch the Wellington bomber being badly coned over to our left; the flak at the apex of the cone was intense. The aircraft was hit, began to burn slowly and then suddenly exploded and fell in flaming pieces to the ground.

I watched and saw all the searchlights quickly transfer their attention to another unfortunate and I began to dwell upon what I'd just seen. It was hard to believe that five men had died in that explosion – their bodies scattered over the Ruhr, never to be found; no funerals, no mourning – just posted as 'missing believed killed on operations against Düsseldorf.'

Then we ourselves began to get involved and I had other things to think about as a shell burst uncomfortably close and we were holed in several places. The whole area was a hive of activity but Calder was as cool as a cucumber. We bombed acurately and left the wasp's nest with all possible speed, which was 125 miles per hour – laughable really!

About this time young Geoffrey Cheshire – brother of the world-famous Group Captain Leonard Cheshire – went missing and we were all upset as he was so popular with the squadron. Group Captain 'Chesh' was terribly upset and had an even stronger desire to hit the enemy – this desire became almost fanatical and quickly led to courageous and daring exploits like coming back from the target at roof-top height and shooting anything that moved at night in Germany. He wasn't shot down, miraculously, and I believe that getting away with it so often led 'Chesh' to adopt these tactics regularly in his highly successful low-level target marking technique. I liked Cheshire enormously, as did we all. I remember once going on a pub-crawl when Cheshire got somewhat high and was sticking pins in his hand without drawing blood. To my surprise, when he taught me the knack I was able to do it too!

My next op was on 28th August with Pilot Officer Kirkpatrick. He was quite experienced and we had an easy target this time – Dunkerque. This was almost worse than the op itself – we knew at 9.30 that morning that we were going to operate that night but of course the target was kept secret till briefing at 12.15 a.m.. Occupying one's mind was a problem; we played snooker, table tennis, cards, and wrote letters – anything to keep one's mind off the impending danger. I frequently used to go for a long walk with Geoff and we chatted away about this and that in a pretence of light-hearted camaraderie.

Looking back, I think it was bad policy for Group Commanders to announce that certain crews would be flying on operations that night. The names went up on a blackboard often as early as 9 a.m. and briefing would not take place until 9 or 10 p.m. with actual take-off at midnight. The target was not announced officially until briefing but such was the 'bush telegraph' on some squadrons that the target was generally known before lunch! Seeing one's name on the board so early left one several hours to brood on the risks and dangers, and frequently some crew members went 'sick' for some reason or another after getting themselves unnecessarily worked up. What a job for the Squadron Medical Officer, who had to decide between malingering and real illness! He had to be able to distinguish beween fear and real headache and make his decision whether to put you off 'sick' or whether to order you to fly. No wonder those capable doctors were good psychologists too!

I would have preferred a method whereby all crews were standing by until Command either decided to operate or stood us down. That way, apprehensions would have existed but if one had not actually been named, one need not have worried so much. I personally always found that when my name went up on the squadron ops board early in the day, I started to get restless and nervous – I would start biting my nails and couldn't put my mind to anything – I even lost my normally good appetite. It meant hanging round the aerodrome sometimes for twelve hours, feeling tensed up and anxious but as soon as I entered the briefing room I would feel better as there were details and things to be memorised and worked on which kept one's mind occupied.

Briefing was an exciting affair! On a 'maximum effort' maybe eighteen or more crews would be assembled (126 aircrew) together; with briefing officers, intelligence officers and all those directly concerned with planning operations. The Station Commander would normally enter first and announce the target. He was then followed by all the specialist officers – meteorological, wireless, navigation, armaments, intelligence and finally the Squadron Commander who would sum up and explain in detail the method of attack, height, timing, etc.. All pilots and navigators would synchronise their watches and with a 'good luck everyone' the crews would disperse. The whole station then buzzed with activity – navigators would be plotting their courses on charts, pilots checking with ground crews any last minute adjustments, the locker rooms filled with boisterous aircrew changing into flying suits, packing escape kits, torches, thermos flasks, boiled sweets, biscuits, 'keep awake' pills, colour cartridges, mascots, empty beer bottles to throw out over Germany (they made a horrible whistle as they fell!) and all the other paraphernalia that we all needed for the task ahead.

At the appointed time 3-ton lorries would assemble outside the locker rooms and convey us out to our aircraft at dispersal points often a mile away, dropping off the various crews at their aircraft. This was the real climax of the day and forced humour or sometimes sheer silence would prevail, depending on how we all felt. There were always the squadron 'wags' who were irrepressible and they would laugh and joke whatever the target – I sometimes wondered whether they had no imagination and were quite fearless, or whether this was a way of unloading their fears. We were all frightened to a degree, but no one showed it, or even dared to indicate his real feelings in public.

As soon as the crews reached their aircraft the real work began, often in darkness and by torchlight. The ground crews would be there to help. Stuff had to be stowed away, guns checked, radios and intercom checked, and the pitot head-cover removed (God help you if you forgot!). This was a nine inch long metal rod, with a hole drilled through the middle, at the end of the wing, which was connected to the airspeed indicator in the cockpit. If you forgot to remove the protective cover you had no airspeed indicator – as simple as that, and yet hundreds of pilots forgot in the excitement of the moment, often to die with their crews as a result of their forgetfulness.

Geoff Thomas once did this with a full bomb and petrol load aboard on a dark night, and he told me he'd never been so terrified when he became airborne at the end of the runway and found his airspeed registering zero! A skilled and experienced pilot would generally cope but it wasn't easy guessing one's speed in the dark on an approach to land. Equally stupid and horrible to watch was one of our pilots who took off in a Halifax with the elevator control locked! He'd failed to carry out a simple but vital check, with the result that they became airborne with a full bomb-load, climbed steeply, stalled, and exploded, killing everyone instantly. It really taught you the vital need for 'cockpit checks' which though tedious and a frightful nuisance, were obviously essential. If you made a mistake or forgot one vital check in thirty, you usually discovered it in the air, by which time it was too late.

I once saw Wing Commander Young take off in a Halifax on a flight test and he suddenly started to bank to port on becoming airborne. The bank became steeper and steeper and I felt sure he was going to crash when suddenly the Halifax straightened up, made a circuit of the aerodrome and landed safely. The airframe fitter had cross-cabled the aileron trimmertabs and David Young hadn't spotted this during his cockpit checks, with the result that to bank to starboard meant using all his enormous strength. Only because he had 3,000 hours flying behind him with Scottish Aviation at Prestwick did he cotton on to this careless mistake, and lived to tear a colossal strip off the fitter responsible!

As pupil pilots we used to chant: 'Ailerons, elevator, rudder, undercarriage locked down, flaps up, pitot head cover removed, compass set. altimeter set at barometric pressure, hatches closed, oxygen off, bomb door closed, oil pressures, airscrews set at fine pitch, intercom working, radio functioning, bombs unfused, brakes efficient, windows clean, all instruments and navigational aids functioning' to name but a few! Anything missed out could mean sudden death or worst, or an abortive operation at best. No wonder they drilled 'cockpit checks' into you from Tiger Moths to Halifaxes.

All checks complete and the engines run up in turn, you signalled to the ground crew 'chocks away' and taxied out to the take-off runway where a final check took place. If all was well you turned into wind, lined up and started the take-off run.

We were driven out to the aircraft at 1 a.m. and made all the vital checks at dispersal point. Kirkpatrick (who was later killed) taxied out at 1.25 a.m. and inadvertently stalled one engine so we had to wait for ages for a heavy starter battery, and didn't take off till 2.15 a.m.. This meant that we would be at the tail end of the bomber stream, but as Dunkerque was not a deep penetration it didn't matter so much. We carried out a glide bombing attack from 15,000 to 11,000 feet in bright moonlight and our bombs definitely straddled the docks. A glide attack quite often deceived the Huns because the engines made no noise and one was losing height all the

Inspecting Michael Renaut's Halifax after operations.

The starlings' nest found after a trip to Brest. The eggs were cold!

time. This tended to fox their radar and more often than not one wasn't fired at.

Dawn broke as we left the target and the sky was quickly lightening so we put our nose down and dived for home, re-crossing the English coast at Orfordness. Just as we crossed the coast we met a Messerschmitt 110 who challenged us with a Very cartridge and then came in to attack. Kirkpatrick dived to tree top level and took violent evading action; I was in the front turret together with one gas-operated Vickers machine-gun and I longed to draw a bead on this bastard in the Me110, but the evasive action was so violent that it felt as if we were on a roller coaster. We shook him off and I vented my rage on a few seagulls. We climbed up to 1,000 feet and entered some strato-cumulus and then got horribly lost somewhere over the Midlands but all turned out OK and we landed at base at 7 a.m..

Geoff and I went back to our flat to sleep and spent a lazy day shopping in Darlington. There we met some other crews who told us that we were operating again and advised us to hurry back for briefing. I couldn't believe that we were to do two ops in twenty-four hours but nevertheless we jumped in the car and tore back. Sure enough we were both down to operate – I with dear old Mercer again, and the target was Frankfurt.

We flew in ideal weather all the way to the target and Mercer allowed me to operate the bombsight and release the bombs. We could see the town beautifully and bombed from 8,000 feet very satisfactorily. Mercer allowed me to fly the Whitley back and instructed me on flak and searchlight evasion when we crossed the enemy coast at Dunkerque. I learnt a lot under his guidance and felt more ready to captain an aircraft, which one was usually allowed to do after eight trips as second pilot. This was my seventh.

My last trip as second pilot was on 2nd September with an Australian called Sergeant Newborn, to Frankfurt again. We had an uneventful trip at 15,000 feet all the way to the target and then got caught in a searchlight belt. Don Newborn let me work the IFF (Identification Friend or Foe) as the transmitter affected the Hun radar, but at the critical moment I collapsed through lack of oxygen. Evidently my oxygen plug was not pushed home fully and I passed out cold! Luckily Newborn, who had done twenty-eight trips, sent someone back down the fuselage when he couldn't get an answer from me over the intercom and they pushed my plug fully home and turned up the oxygen supply. I soon recovered and dropped our bombs and leaflets plumb in the middle of the town, which wasn't difficult in the perfect visibility and conditions. The effect of dropping leaflets was questionable. Whether the German civilian population took them seriously any more than we believed their 'Lord Haw Haw' I find a difficult question to answer. Anyway we scattered millions and millions of leaflets over the German Reich so they were never short of lavatory paper!

Something went very wrong with the navigation coming home (I was doing the flying) and with fierce easterly winds blowing up we crossed the English coast at Southampton instead of Orfordness! Newborn wouldn't risk crossing the coast at that point so he made me fly all the way round the Kentish coast and across the Thames estuary till we crossed the coast on our designated point in Essex. I began to look at the petrol tank readings where the needles were hovering on zero and so did Newborn. We eventually joined the circuit at Cottesmore aerodrome but so did a number of other planes and we were held in circuit for three-quarters of an hour (almost like London Airport today!). The petrol tank needles had been wavering on zero for too long and as I put the aircraft down on the runway we ran out of petrol completely. This was a dangerous situation because we were stationary in the middle of the runway with not even enough petrol to taxi to safety, but as we pondered on our plight a Hampden came in to land behind us and we prepared to flee to safety, he too, ran out of petrol and came to a halt some two hundred yards behind us. We had been airborne for eight hours and forty minutes.

I had now completed eight trips as second pilot and I knew that the next operation would be my 'fresher' as it was called, as captain of aircraft. I had done 260 hours. This was really comparatively little to be entrusted with a heavy bomber and five human lives but I felt strangely confident and almost fearless at the thought. I hoped and prayed that I would be given an easy target like Ostend, but it was not to be and on the 13th September (thank God I was not superstitious!) the target was announced as Brest with briefing at 5 o'clock that afternoon. I had a long and weary wait but there was eager anticipation and not fear in me. There was, and always would be, the flutter in the pit of one's stomach but it was controllable and I certainly didn't think that my end had come.

Take-off was at 8.30 p.m. All went smoothly and I had taken the usual pill to keep me awake. We climbed slowly to 15,000 feet over Southern England but I felt hot and sleepy – the immediate reaction of the pill was sleepiness – and ill at ease.

Suddenly I heard a voice over the intercom saying, 'Are you all right, Skipper?' and I awoke startled and self conscious. I had actually fallen asleep and let the aircraft lose height in a dive to 8,000 feet.

I hastily reassured my crew that I was all right and told them we had been caught in a colossal air pocket. I shall never know whether they believed me or not! We crossed the Channel and altered course for Brest and later we could see the defence barrage, as it was such a clear night.

I began my long bombing run from seaward and immediately we came under heavy fire from the shore batteries and ships and we were hit in numerous places. This was unnerving as I never knew Brest was so heavily defended – nor had they warned us at briefing – but presumably the Huns had berthed some battle-cruisers in the docks and their armament was contributing largely to the barrage.

There were night fighters about and we saw Sergeant Bell shoot down a Heinkel 112 over the target, it was the first German aircraft I had seen shot down at night and this flaming, falling ball of fire was awe-inspiring. However, we had no time to stare as we were still under continuous fire but we bombed fairly accurately and plastered the dock area. This was enough for me and I dived steeply seawards to avoid the flak, very pleased to have come through with thirty-five holes in the old Whitley and to know that we hadn't been hit in the petrol tanks or engines nor had any crew injuries as a result.

I levelled out some miles over the sea and was in quite a tizzy at the thought that I'd done my first trip as captain. Down went the thermos of coffee and the intercom bristled with excited small talk as we made our way homewards discussing what we were all going to do when we got back to base. We landed after seven hours exactly, were de-briefed and fed, and crawled into bed happy and contented at the first obstacle having been overcome. 'Debriefing' was simply a formality where all crew members were interrogated after an 'op' by an intelligence officer.

The sort of questions he asked were: 'Did you bomb the target, If not, what and where did you bomb? Did you observe the results? Did you have any combat with night fighters? Did you damage or shoot down any enemy fighters, and if so, what type? Did you see any of our aircraft shot down; if so, when, where, and did you see anyone abandon by parachute? What were the flak concentrations like? Were they any better or worse than our intelligence had indicated? Did you see anything unusual?'

All the debriefing reports were gathered in, analysed and sent to Group HQ. They in turn checked all the different squadrons' details and forwarded them to Bomber Command. Then the Intelligence branch sorted out the corn from the chaff and an accurate picture emerged. From this it was possible to correct our estimations of their flak batteries, determine how many night fighters had been bagged, corroborate and confirm 'unusual events'. If several crews reported the same 'hallucination' at the same time and in the same place, some credence usually attached to their reports. I recall once reporting seeing a Messerschmitt 262 jet fighter near Berlin and our Intelligence officer seemed sceptical – he then made me have doubts because I only saw it for an instant and wasn't absolutely certain, and none of my crew saw it. However, Bomber Command interpreted all the de-briefing reports that night and their Lancaster crews had reported seeing a fighter resembling the Me262 in the same area, at the same time. It was possible to establish therefore that this night fighter *was* in service and could be regarded with extreme caution!

The next morning I went out to the Whitley to inspect the damage from flak and I was surprised at the number of holes near vital parts. The ground crew were already patching up and putting in new panels when someone shouted: 'Look what I've found!' and there, under the starboard wing, was an airframe fitter carefully pulling out a starling's nest with five eggs. The birds had built their nest inside the wing where the tethering flap was open and had, I suppose, built the nest since 26th August, when the aircraft last flew. The dispersal point was in a field and the starlings had evidently thought that this huge, black shape was there for their benefit. The eggs were cold, of course, and no doubt the starlings had baulked at accompanying us to Brest.

On 20th September I did my second 'fresher' to Ostend, and I quote from my diary:

> Very easy trip. Bombed on E. to W. heading without interference from ground defences. 4 hours 40 minutes airborne.

Others were not so lucky, and poor Jock McLeod and his crew were killed that night. It was his first 'fresher'.

The 'fresher' target for German bomber crews was Hull, in Yorkshire. They chose this for the same reasons that we chose Ostend, Dunkerque and Brest – it was easy to find at night and did not involve deep penetration over enemy territory. Poor Hull came in for pretty constant battering during the period 1940-1944 and was in fact, by population per square mile, the most heavily bombed town in the whole of Britain.

The time was drawing near for my 21st birthday and I began to look forward to the party – I was a true 'Michael' for I had been born on Michaelmas Day, the 29th September. In the morning of the great day I stood to attention in Squadron Leader Mercer's office and asked for the day and night off duty. I'll always remember his reply: 'No chance, Renaut; you're operating tonight like everyone else. Sorry.'

That shattered me and I returned to the crew-room somewhat dejected, to see my name on the board as captain. I could already see the headline: 'Pilot missing believed killed on his twenty-first birthday.'

Briefing was early and the target was named as Stettin and my heart fell. This was a deep penetration into Germany and a heavily defended target near the Baltic. I entered in my diary: 'My twenty-first birthday. What a glorious way to spend an evening.'

We took off at 9.30 p.m. and it was bitterly cold at altitude. The alcohol froze in the compass and the hot coffee froze as we drank it. It was a long and tedious North Sea crossing and we crossed the Danish coast after about 3¾ hours flying. The flak was intermittent as our route took us carefully through the Baltic and avoided defended areas. It was a perfect starlit night with no moon and thanks to the conditions my navigator had an easy job routing us

safely to Stettin (actually in Poland). The town was burning well on
our arrival and our bomb-load was dropped bang in the middle of
the blaze.

Ominously the flak was conspicuous by its absence and we knew
night fighters were prowling the area. Sure enough, as we left the
target area we had an Me109 come in to attack. Thanks to the clear
night sky, we spotted him in good time and with no bombs on
board we were able to fling the Whitley about all over the sky. Later
on over Denmark we spotted a Ju88 but thank God he never saw us.

My relief at re-crossing the North Sea without either danger or
trouble was inexpressible and I quickly lost height down to a
warmer level. I had been frozen stiff over the target and couldn't
feel either my feet or my hands – the second and third fingers on
each hand were absolutely white and numb. To this day, when I am
particularly cold these same two fingers go numb and white and I
wonder whether this afflication dates from Michaelmas night in
1941. My God, I was cold! Though I was too afraid to admit it to
anyone for fear of being ragged, I secretly wore long woollen
combinations for my tour of ops as my knees always used to get so
cold! I also had woollen mittens, silk gloves and fleece-lined
gauntlets, but still my fingers were numb with cold, and my feet I
just never felt for hours at a time. I must have suffered from bad
circulation – for other aircrews were able to keep warm.

One night we were briefed for a trip to Essen with take-off at
midnight and our Station Commander routed us straight through
the heavy defended area, instead of round it, because 90 mile-an-
hour tail winds would give us a ground speed of 250 mph. It worked
well and we flew through the flak barrage unscathed – I remember
well we were at 16,000 feet, bitterly cold and going like the clappers
when I suddenly wanted to pee very badly. I think it was a
combination of too much coffee, nervous tension and extreme
cold.

Anyway, I had no second pilot and I had to ask the flight engineer
to bring me the pee bottle whilst I struggled out of my seat at the
controls, leaving 'George', the automatic pilot to fly the aeroplane.
This was a dangerous thing to do if a night fighter attacked but I had
no option – I was bursting. With numb fingers I struggled through
layers of clothing and held the bottle somewhat unsteadily. To aim

accurately was impossible, and my poor navigator, who was down below at his table, was showered with frozen urine falling as sleet on to his maps! I was laughing so much at his indignation that my aim became even poorer and it seemed to go on for minutes. What ecstatic relief as I hurried back to my seat!

The Whitley had the usual heating system but it only blew cold air in terribly cold conditions and there was literally no means of keeping warm, not even with fur-lined boots and fleecy-lined, heated, Sidcot suit. At my request my mother had knitted me some woollen knee covers but even those had no effect. We landed exhausted 9 hours 25 minutes after take-off and I felt too tired even to enjoy the coffee and rum and the inevitable bacon and egg.

Although we didn't realise it at the time, these long trips were a frightful strain; on really deep penetrations, such as Magdeburg, one could be the victim of Hun defences for four or five hours at a stretch. There were, of course, long stretches of countryside like the Black Forest where one might have been flying over the Atlantic, it was so quiet. But quiet or not, the strain remained and whilst there were no guns firing there was always the risk of fighter attack. The eye-strain was colossal in the ever constant watch on the night sky. One had also to beware of hallucinations and 'seeing things'; I can recall one night a pilot at de-briefing reported seeing barrage balloons at 18,000 feet! When he was told that these were puffs of black smoke left hanging in the sky by heavy flak he refused to believe it. We tried hard to convince him that this would mean a cable 3½ miles long but he remained adamant and said: 'They *were* balloons!'

I was sympathetic because I'd been caught myself on two occasions – the first was when I was flying just above a bed of stratus cloud on the way back from Nuremburg and I suddenly saw a night fighter coming straight for me with his wing lamp full on. I dived into a cloud and told the crew to keep their eyes skinned. A minute later I nosed cautiously up out of the cloud and there he was nearer than ever – neither of the gunners had seen him. Back down again I went into the cloud and on the second surfacing I realised that it was the moon coming up over the cloud bank! I did feel a lemon but nevertheless I'd frightened myself to death over it.

The second occasion was when I took violent evasive action from an oncoming night fighter only to find that it was a squashed fly on the windscreen! Shadows also cast weird shapes on a cloud bank – there could be one's own shadow or that of another aircraft and on a dark night one could imagine almost anything and be convinced it was real.

On 5th October 1941 I went sent to No 2 Blind Approach Training Course at Driffield (one of the few bomber stations in Yorkshire which had been severely attacked by the Hun) for six days. One of the instructors was Flying Officer Ennis who was universally known as 'Ennis the menace', but was a brilliant pilot. We used to take off and land in thick fog purely by instruments and team flying and it certainly gave one confidence in the system. There was a steady hum in one's ears down the centre of the beam but if one drifted off to starboard one heard intermittent dashes and if one drifted to port one heard intermittent dots. With this system it was possible to take off and land with twenty yards visibility and Ennis taught me a lot. The course covered thirty hours flying. Instrument flying was often eerie because one's own instincts told one one's altitude and one's instrument another, and yet one could rely implicitly on the instruments – but it took infinite faith. Poor Ennis was later killed on the successful raid on Peenemünde.

'Peenemünde' was both a major success and major tragedy. Our Intelligence knew that the German scientists were well ahead with the development of guided missiles and it was essential to retard the programme with a devastating raid on the development centre – this small town of Peenemünde, on the Baltic. Our Intelligence misled Bomber Command as to the number of flak concentrations which, they claimed, were scattered and a few in number; they failed to establish the fact that the Hun realising the importance of this work, had moved in large quantities of both light and heavy flak to guard the aerodrome.

In consequence of this, Bomber Harris and his staff planned the operation at a comparatively low level, with the result that the main force met with the most fiendish and concentrated flak and the bombers were decimated. It was a credit to the bomber crews that they pressed home their attack with extraordinary accuracy despite the frightful loss of lives. On the credit side, Peenemünde was badly damaged, key scientists were killed, vital equipment and prototype 'V' weapons were destroyed and their VI and V2 development programme was retarded for several months. Londoners could thank Bomber Command for the fact that flying bombs didn't appear until mid-1944 and V2 rockets some months later. Had the raid not been so successful, the duration of the war, or even the course of events, might have been so very different.

It was after this course that I was given a new navigator – Pilot Officer Collins – and he was terrific! He'd been at Oxford and could play simultaneously six games of chess blindfolded and win every game. We called him 'The Professor' and no other nickname could have suited him better. I grew to admire this man; I respected his enormous brain and when I visited him in his London flat and met his lovely and attractive wife, we were closer than ever. A pilot and his navigator were the closest members of a bomber crew and in our case we were inseparable.

Tim Collins undoubtedly shepherded me through my first tour of operations. He always kept in touch with me after our first tour of thirty-five operations, and I had a letter from him saying that he had gone back on his second tour of ops with a young inexperienced pilot. His letter said: 'If we get through our first five trips with this pilot we'll be OK but I'm a bit nervous as to his ability.' They lasted three trips, and were shot down over Germany. Nothing was ever heard of any member of the Halifax crew and I felt desolated at the news. I imagine a night fighter got them and they exploded or crashed into the sea, never to be seen or heard of again.

There followed on 12th and 14th October two operations to Nuremburg and these were deep penetrations into Germany. We always seemed to be routed between Dunkerque and Ostend and I was amazed that the Hun didn't move some flak batteries into the gap. If one's navigation was accurate and one passed at a point equidistant between the two, the searchlights and flak were almost negligible, but they were bad if one passed over and not between. One could almost say that if you passed over you passed on! Strangely enough neither of these ops made a clear impression on my mind and for that reason they must both have been trouble-free except I see from my diary that we landed at Abingdon after the first and at Swanton Morley after the second. That indicated that we must have been short of petrol, but not lost, as I had Tim Collins as navigator.

On 24th October we moved as 78 Squadron to Croft – a new

aerodrome just built and just over the borders of Yorkshire. I hated it as it was a satellite aerodrome, all Nissen huts, and dear old Middleton St George was a permanent brick-built station and eminently comfortable. Geoff and I unpacked and shared a room in one of the huts and when we climbed into bed on the first night we could feel the damp bed clothes literally absorbing our body heat – I knew this was fatal and I woke up the very next morning with a severe chill.

The next day one of our Whitleys crashed on take-off and somersaulted on to its back, killing all the crew except the wireless operator. He, poor chap, was trapped upside down in his seat but quite unhurt and full of beans. The Medical Officer kept him cheerful while an army of fitters began the job of extricating him. This was not easy because petrol was everywhere and the smallest spark would have blown up the entire aeroplane and its occupants.

After six hours of delicate kicking and cutting, breaking and bending, the poor chap was released and made straight for the Sergeants' Mess to get himself a stiff whisky. Before he even drank, he collapsed and died and I had my first experience of death from shock. It rather stunned us all that a man with no injuries and talking excitedly to his saviours could suddenly collapse and die, but he did and I'll never forget his courage. What he must have gone through in those six hours no one will every know but he must have realised from the pungent smell of petrol that the least spark would have killed him. Was this fear? I'm convinced it was – fear of fire, fear of the losing battle in freeing him, fear of his crew dead all round him, and it was fear that killed him without leaving a trace.

I recovered from my chill and on 1st November my name went up on the ops boards at 9.30 a.m. Kiel was the target, not a very nice one from experience, and somewhat unhealthy when it comes to flak. Fate was on our side and after three-quarters of an hour's flying my radio packed up and we had to return to base. It was on this operation that Squadron Leader Mercer failed to return, and I dwelt upon how lucky I was not to have been his second pilot. The loss of Mercer became a fear and a worry – what were my chances of survival if an experienced man like Mercer went for a burton? It taught me the risks that I already knew were one in a hundred on survival and it wasn't a cheering thought.

CHAPTER III

Operational on Halifaxes

I didn't fly again till 5th December. I was posted to No 28 Halifax Conversion Course at Leconfield where I learned to fly the larger four-engined Halifax. I had a very good instructor – Flight Lieutenant Owen – and I soloed after an hour and a quarter's dual. The Halifax was a tough aircraft and could take a lot of knocking about from flak and fighters; it was not as pretty or as gentle as the Lancaster but I vastly preferred it in battle. Great hunks could be shot away and still the Halifax plodded on undismayed. It was at Leconfield that I first met Willie Tait – the man who later sank the *Tirpitz* – and had some dual instruction from him. He was very quiet and shy and according to the mechanics was an excellent pilot, except for his landings which were well known as bumpy. It is incredible to think that this shy young man won the DSO four times.

I had rather a shock that week when Flight Lieutenant Owen killed himself and thirteen other men. What happened apparently was that Owen was airtesting a Halifax on a blustery, rainy day: he had offered a trip to sundry fitters and clerks and they were following a railway line in poor visibility (known as 'Bradshawing') when they flew into a hillside. The Halifax exploded killing all the occupants instantly. There was a hell of a row about it because several unauthorised personnel were on board and none was entered in the flight manifest. The result was that there had to be a Station roll-call to try and establish who was missing. One must remember that in a crash like this it was impossible to identify twenty-eight arms and legs and fourteen trunks and heads.

The Halifax had a tendency to swing on take-off in inexperienced hands and therefore the emphasis was on take-offs and landings. I found the brute quite placid, I enjoyed flying the type and of course there was the extra security of four engines. However, there were twice as many dials as on the Whitley and this meant that one carried a flight engineer to look after most of them, just leaving the pilot to his essential instruments. We then had Rolls Royce Merlin engines and they suffered all types of coolant leaks; later we were to have Bristol Hercules radial engines and these were to transform the Halifax into a fine aeroplane. I treasure my painting of a Halifax Mark III, signed for me very kindly by the late Sir Frederick Handley-Page. I often used to go to Radlett aerodrome where Handley-Page Halifaxes were collected and flown to operational squadrons and I found Sir Frederick a kind and charming man. I certainly had faith in his aeroplane.

On 22nd December I was posted to No 76 Squadron, Middleton St George. It felt queer returning to the station. The command of the squadron had been given to Wing Commander David Young, DSO, DFC, AFC, and I was to meet him for the first time. What an incredible person he was – tall, good-looking, with iron-grey hair, a devout Catholic, an experienced pilot with already 3,000 hours mainly in civil flying behind him. A man of extreme courage and a true 'commander'. He oozed authority and the impact he made on the squadron and the station was electric – here was a man who could be depended upon. Our Station Commander was a lovable man – Goup Captain Tommy Traill (later to achieve fame in 2nd TAF as Air Marshal) and he and David Young got on well together. Before embarking on this book I wrote to David Young (who now lives in Leighton Buzzard) and asked him if he could let me have any details he could remember of our war together and he wrote me a long letter in reply. To let one judge the man I quote from his letter:

'My dear Mike, you flatter me by asking for any memories that I may have of our war years together in order to help you with your book. After twenty years I find it a little difficult to respond with the swift and accurate reactions we had in those days. I am getting past middle-age! Be very sure that I do not wish to be quoted; it is your book not mine. I am writing just as I might talk and I may perhaps reveal some incident that you did not know about and I may certainly reveal some of my fears of those days. There was nothing unique about them and they are probably the same as yours were. What is fear? No one has described it as I know it. Once over Kiel I was coned badly and being shot at terribly and we lost height from 10,000 feet down to 600 feet. I was concentrating on instrument flying and was not conscious of anyone else in the aeroplane. Did I shut out fear? I don't think so; I was scared all right but the panic of the rear gunner, someone much younger than I, made me assert my authority instinctively and without thought and in doing so to get a firmer grip on myself.

'Fear! – I remember another young pilot, a charming and gallant lad of twenty or so. He was my second pilot on a trip to Düsseldorf – his first trip. Things got a bit sticky, what with concentrated flak and searchlights. I was paying attention to the bombing-run and then on getting clear of the target area when I turned round to see how the boy was reacting. Absolutely deadpan as he caught my eye so I thought, "He'll do" and got on with the job. Later it turned out that he was as frightened as I was but neither of us knew it and he refused to believe me when I said I was very frightened. I was a hero to that boy, because he didn't believe me when I said that I had felt frightened! He went round the squadron saying: "What a man the Wingco is – in the middle of all that flak and stuff over Düsseldorf I looked at him and have never seen such an expression of fiendish delight in anyone. He looked really happy and I was scared stiff!" Poor boy – he died, as so many others, before he lost his illusions.

'The daylight raid on Heraklion (Crete) when you and Hank Iveson put up such a good show. I did not see it because the Station Commander was on leave and I had to take command. When he got back I recommended a bar to your DFC and he said: "Nonsense – who led the other squadron? I'll put him up for one."

'I remember Rufforth near York, the dances and the little nurse that you fell for so suddenly after never having any interest in wenches? Do you remember the horrible crashes? Two Halifaxes colliding in perfect visibility a couple of miles to the south. The one from Marston Moor in which the elevator control fell apart for lack of a split-pin and it dived straight into the ground on the edge of Rufforth. Do you recall the night when a pupil crashed on a farmhouse, no-one knew why, it was nowhere in the line of approach? God, what a blaze! The roof fell in and someone went upstairs and got an old man out who was unconscious. Someone said his wife was still there so I went up myself and could find no one in the smoke so I went down again just in time because the stairs caught fire. A few minutes later the old man came to life and said his wife was in the bed. Len Steele, the farmer's son, climbed up a drainpipe got in and found her and then had to wait at the window until the ladder arrived. Undoubtedly she would have died if he had not held her at the window for those few minutes and I was very glad to hear later that he had got the George Medal on my recommendation. It was very well deserved. Here are a few memories – draw from them as you will.'

In mid-December I suddenly heard that I was to be commissioned (on Squadron Leader Mercer's recommendation) and off I dashed to see Moss Bros in London to get kitted out. They had such a choice of sizes that I had no difficulty in being fitted from stock and back and I went to Middleton St George feeling very proud. That day one of the Halifax crews was executing a rate four turn on take-off (exhibitionism and very dangerous) when the wingtip touched the ground and the Halifax cart-wheeled and exploded. A number of us rushed to the scene to give assistance but the heat of the blaze repelled us and we could only stand and watch seven men incinerated. I shall never forget the sight of the second pilot trying to hack his way feverishly out of the cabin but he screamed as the blaze overcame him and he perished. I felt slightly sick, but in other ways I had become callous at the sight of death and although that face haunted me for days I soon forgot the incident.

However, what I didn't forget was Group Captain Tommy Traill's request to me to meet the parents at Darlington Station and accompany them to the funeral. This was my first job as an officer and I was nervous as to whether I would do it well. I met the parents off the train at Darlington, together with the fiancée of the dead pilot who was carrying a large parcel under her arm, and escorted them to the aerodrome. The young girl asked me whether she could put her wedding-dress in the coffin and she particularly wanted to do it personally. I told her it was best to remember him as he was and not to look at the ghastly mess in the coffin but she insisted and was crying desperately. It was a harrowing sight – this girl sobbing her heart out – I felt quite helpless and on the verge of tears myself. I knew that there were only sandbags (as makeweight) and charred flesh in the coffin and I simply didn't know how to dissuade her.

I eventually asked the station padre to come to my aid and he finally managed to quieten her and persuade her to let us do it. I gave the three of them lunch and after about four hours of tears I took them back to Darlington Station and saw them off. The father said to me: 'Thank you for your kindness; if the circumstances were not so tragic, we could almost have enjoyed ourselves.' So I felt I had done the job adequately and that my attempts at humour had not been in vain.

I had the greatest respect for the RAF Meteorological branch – they had an exceedingly difficult task, not only on operational squadrons but on Conversion units also. It was their task to try and forecast the weather conditions over England and as far away as Czechoslovakia with as much accuracy as possible. Some ops lasted ten hours or more and, needless to say, our English weather could change completely in four hours, let alone ten. I well remember one night in 1941 the weather over England changing so quickly that although we left in clear starlit skies and a strongly easterly wind, on our return some eight hours later, the whole of Yorkshire, Lincoln-shire and Norfolk was blanketed with thick fog. The petrol carried did not permit a diversion to Prestwick or Devon, so some thirty Whitleys baled out their crews over Yorkshire, the aircraft being all completely destroyed yet not one member of 150 aircrew was killed or even injured. In later years we had emergency runways 2½ miles long at Marston, Carnaby and Woodridge and these were fitted with 'FIDO' fog dispersal equipment. These consisted of dozens of petrol lamps on each side of the runway which, when lit, cleared a path through the fog. This saved countless bombers in 1943-1945.

We had a young Met officer at Rufforth, ginger-haired and nervous, and I tried hard for several weeks to get him to fly with me. He was frightened of flying but I eventually persuaded him one fine June evening to come on a short flip round York. I went out to my Halifax and only took a flight engineer and this Met officer with me. When we got airborne I circled York Minster at 850 feet and let him look around at the landmarks and whilst his attention was focussed elsewhere I quickly stopped the two starboard engines and 'feathered' the airscrews. The Met Officer suddenly noticed the two engines had stopped and was quite panic-stricken and kept pointing at them and saying – 'Are we all right?'

It was naughty of me but I was very schoolboyish and my practical joke nearly misfired because as I approached to land on two engines, the port wing suddenly caught fire at 400 feet for no apparent reason!! This left me with one engine only and I had to do a glide approach and landing. I pressed the Graviner fire extinguisher as soon as we touched down and the fire immediately subsided. Needless to say, the Met Officer's flight baptism was the first and last time he ever got airborne!

We had a visit of six Russian officers who had distinguished themselves in the early campaign against Germany. I was to act as host to a Major Svetsov, and I found him a very likable man. He actually played snooker, and, such was my knowledge of Russians, that I thought they'd never heard of the game! The Officers Mess food was luxurious and the Russians fed like fighting cocks but beneath it all they were accusing us of stuffing ourselves while people in Russia were starving. Had we known it we would have fed them on corned beef and stewed prunes but I doubt if this would have convinced them! For four days we were blanketed with fog and they kept asking us why we weren't attacking the Hun. When we explained that none of our aircraft could land back at base they scoffed and said that if we lost the whole squadron what did it matter! It was attacking the Hun that was most important. I was quite relieved when they departed and I was again able to sit down to roast duck without a guilt complex.

We then had a very unexpected visit from the Duke of Kent. I was asked by Group Captain Traill to assemble all the available crews down at the locker room. Practically the whole squadron were doing a daylight raid on Brest and I wasn't included as I hadn't enough experience of formation flying. I was introduced to the Duke who was most charming, and promptly asked me whether I used brakes on take-off to correct swing! I thought to myself 'What a clever question' but decided on reflection that he'd probably been briefed on the sort of question to ask! I then had lunch with him and Group Captain Traill, which was a great honour and afterwards we stood round the anteroom fire telling stories until it was time for him to leave. Poor man, he was killed soon afterwards as a passenger in a Sunderland when the aircraft flew into a Scottish mountainside. A tragic loss of a fine man!

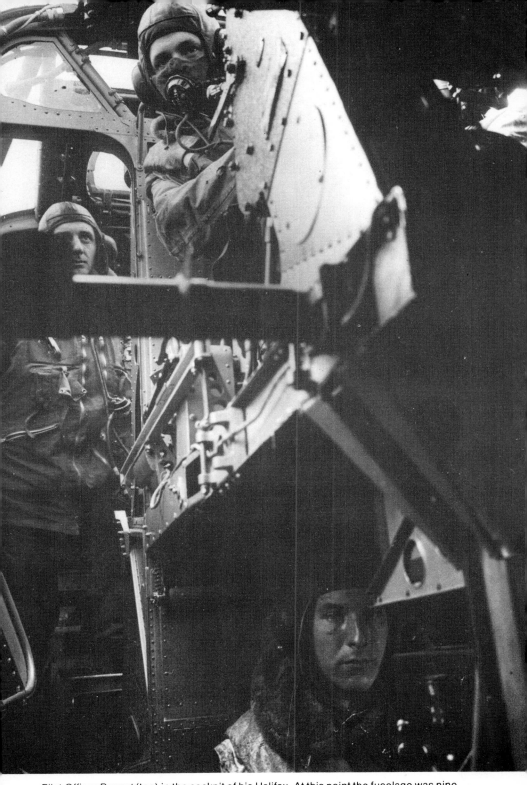

Pilot Officer Renaut (top) in the cockpit of his Halifax. At this point the fuselage was nine foot deep. The wireless operator is sitting in his cubby-hole below the pilot and the flight engineer standing behind.

Michael Renaut (flat cap) with Bill Kofoed, the gallant New Zealander.

During the few days before Christmas 1941 our Intelligence service reported that the cruisers *Scharnhorst* and *Gneisenau* were likely to make a dash for it through the English Channel and all crews were ordered to stay in the locker room in full flying kit. This scare lasted over Christmas and we none of us had any Christmas dinner.

My first operation as a Halifax captain was not until 11th February and the target was Mannheim. Again this was a deep penetration and I wasn't awfully bucked at the idea, particularly when at briefing they warned us that Mannheim was very heavily defended. It was bitterly cold that night and I knew we were in for a cold trip. I felt the security of four engines but looking out at the exhaust flames was somewhat shattering after the old Whitleys – and it all seemed so much bigger. After crossing the enemy coast we had an uneventful trip down south, and it was a glorious starry night so Tim Collins had a nice easy piece of navigation, only having to check by map-reading occasionally.

I was following Mercer's advice and was weaving all the time and throttling the engines out of phase to confuse the enemy radar. We could see the reception committee at Mannheim quite clearly and it looked most unhealthy. On our bombing run we were hit quite badly by flak and my port outer engine must have had a piece of shrapnel through an oil pipe for the oil pressure began to fall off alarmingly. Tim was busy with the Sperry bombsight but I was madly trying to keep a straight course and deal with the failing engine. I was forced to feather the airscrew and thought to myself, 'Oh God, we're only on three engines now.' God forbid a fighter attack or more flak, because I was going to have to nurse back the Halifax on three engines for a very long way.

We bombed very accurately in the centre of the town where all the fires were, and immediately turned round and set course for home. I was making about 150 miles per hour on three engines and as luck would have it there was a dense layer of cloud at 13,000 feet so I simply sat on top of the cloud layer and put the automatic pilot, 'George', in. My rear gunner reported a Junkers 88 night fighter on the starboard quarter but he didn't see us and sheared off after about half a minute.

I sighed deeply after the awful silence and felt so relieved that we'd not been spotted. Flying above a cloud layer was pretty safe as I've said before, but it meant that anyone flying above would spot us easily. Clouds were strange things but terribly beautiful on a moonlight night, especially the towering cumulonimbus. The strato-cumulus was like a layer of cotton wool and one could even practise landing on the layer!

My flight engineer was watching the dials like a hawk and I kept on checking the petrol consumption with him but it appears that on three engines one used less petrol, even though the good engines were revving slightly higher. We-recrossed the enemy coast at the favourite spot and were shot at badly, but soon dived down over the North Sea and made for home. The trip lasted seven hours thirty-five minutes and we were all quite tired and ready for bed. This was my fourteenth trip and I started cutting notches on my locker door – the fitters and airframe mechanics used to paint one small bomb below the pilot's side window for every trip completed in the aircraft. One began to start counting now how many more trips before being 'screened' (finishing thirty trips).

Two days later we attacked Cologne and again had a fairly uneventful trip apart from the rough handling over the Ruhr. An amusing thing happened coming back – I let the second pilot, Sergeant Morris, fly the best part of the return journey and whilst we changed seats I asked him not to be so clumsy. His great bum had knocked the throttles all over the shop and let the flaps partly down! Anyway we changed seats and I was keeping a look out for night fighters when after about ten minutes I suddenly saw a green light on our starboard side. It eventually struck me that all our navigation lights were on – Sergeant Morris had been so clumsy climbing into the seat that his leg had accidentally knocked the navigation light switch. To think that for ten minutes our navigation lights were on! . . . We were literally advertising our presence to night fighters.

It was now my turn to show Morris how to avoid flak and I taught him as Mercer and Cheshire had taught me. We crossed the enemy coast in Holland as arranged and the flak was not very severe – the whole trip lasted six hours.

We were suddenly all assembled next day for a talk on security by Group Captain Traill, the Station Commander, and he impressed upon us that no information should be given away either by letter or verbally. He then proceeded to read extracts from our letters home and I felt most embarrassed when part of a letter of mine was read out. I'd written to my mother telling her that on my first trip in a Halifax I had returned from Mannheim on three engines. I couldn't see any harm in this but we were made to understand that no information should be given away at all. Telephone lines were tapped, letters were opened, conversations were listened to – all in an endeavour to stop leakages of information to the enemy. It was a well known fact that at a restaurant called Betty's Bar in York and at the Half Moon pub one could learn the 'Target for Tonight' at ten o'clock in the morning of the operation! That was why on occasions both establishments were put out of bounds to all ranks.

It was during this month that the German battle-cruisers made their dash up the Channel, and on the morning of their escape, during lunch in the mess, we were suddenly rushed out to our aeroplanes. Armourers were busy bombing up with armour-piercing bombs and they'd hardly finished when we were off. There was no briefing – our instructions were simply to find the ships and bomb them. The weather was foul over the Channel and the cloudbase was about 1,200 feet, but we started a square search out in the murk in the hope that we'd locate them. We carried on up and down, until our petrol supply ran out but we never saw anything of them. In fact for four hours we scanned the Channel for ships and never even saw another aeroplane or even a seagull. And yet somewhere in the murk a squadron of Swordfish perished one by one in suicidal torpedo attacks – and we never saw a living soul.

On 21st February we were briefed for a dawn attack on Lister aerodrome in Norway. This was the aerodrome from which the Huns provided air cover for their ships. It was snowing hard on take-off and we flew through severe icing till our ceiling of 9,000 feet and set course for Norway. What happened I shall never know, because we were recalled when halfway across the North Sea and the whole trip was abandoned. Whether the ships had sailed further north, or what, God above knew.

I very nearly crashed on return from this trip; when I circled the aerodrome in the early dawn it was completely snow-covered and one had great difficulty in even spotting the runway. I made my approach in the normal way and then started to hold off for a landing and simply stalled! It was so tricky landing on a blanket of snow that I was attempting to land some eighty feet above the runway. I banged the throttles open to go round again but I hit the runway very hard and ballooned fifty feet in the air. I eventually came to rest after one of the worst landings I've ever made. That taught me to be careful about snow.

We had a pilot in the squadron named Flight Lieutenant Sam Weller who was wonderful. He was short and thick-set and always wore a colossal grin. He had a marvellous sense of humour and even though things may have been hard, Sam was always laughing and joking. He had a habit (one I didn't relish much) of saying at the 'last supper': 'I think you're going to get the chop tonight, Mike.' He was an asset to the squadron and although I don't think he was fearless he certainly never gave the hint that he was anything but. One night he had an entirely new crew with him and for once he kept a straight face but half-way down the runway, with full petrol and bombload, he suddenly said to the crew: 'Do I push the stick forward or back to take off?' The second pilot looked at him in blank amazement and wondered what sort of a captain he'd got. Nobody knows what the other members of the crew thought, but I'll wager they wondered who was at the controls! The more hazardous the target the more old Sam beamed – he was a tonic to us all. I believe he now flies for Scandinavian Air Services.

Wing Commander Young had a similarly fearless outlook although he hadn't Sam Weller's sense of fun – he was after all a commander and had to set an example, so it was different. But Young was a brave man – I remember when he led the squadron on a daylight raid on the German battle-cruisers at Brest. Most of the Stirling Squadron which could only climb to 11,000 feet were shot down by heavy and accurate flak, and even the Halifaxes at 16,000 feet were slowly being decimated by the dense flak. Wing Commander Young was determined not to be put off by the frightening sight of the flak barrage, so he simply lowered his seat in order not to be able to see out of the windows! He made his bombing run on instruments with the rest of the formation clinging close, and on instructions of the bomb-aimer. He claims this was not bravery, but a combination of Catholic faith, and cold calculated flying! he was awarded the DFC for this raid and, we all thought, deservedly.

It was about this time that I had a slight difference of opinion with Wing Commander Young. My particular Halifax at the time, unlike any others I had flown, tended to swing to port on take-off and I was sure it wasn't 'pilot error'. (I had had one narrow escape with two 4,000 lb bombs on board, when I only just cleared the water tower at the far end of the runway; I had to use all the power on the port side to correct the swing and even brakes, but to no avail and I hauled the Halifax off the end of the runway at a mere 90 mph.) I reported this to Wing Commander Young who was adamant that it was the pilot and not the aeroplane! I even argued with him, which was silly as he quite rightly lost his temper with me.

However, one night I was stood down for some reason and another pilot and crew were to use my <u>Halifax 'L for London'</u>. I warned the pilot of what to expect and instead of going to bed I went along at 1.15 a.m. to watch the squadron take-off, out of sheer curiosity. It was cold and I was standing at the end of the runway watching Halifax after Halifax take off with full bomb loads. Eventually 'L for London' lined up and I watched intently as the aeroplane began to lumber down the runway. I could hear the hiss of air as brakes were applied and twice the Halifax veered left off the runway on to the grass and back. The pilot was evidently in difficulty and at the far end of the runway there was an awful bang and the Halifax seemed to haul itself off the ground, its engines thundering and sparks flying from it. Miraculously it gained height and slowly circled the aerodrome at 100 feet making an eerie roar.

I didn't wait a moment but grabbed a car and raced round the perimeter track to the far end of the take-off runway. There was confusion and panic at a dispersal point where my 'L for London' had crashed through a metal gantry, shattered a groundcrew hut and shed its undercarriage by a hedgerow! We got some torches and followed the path of the Halifax across a ploughed field where we found parts of the metal airscrews (8 inches long and at least a dozen from the four-bladed tips). We also found undercarriage nacelle doors and sundry other pieces of the aircraft and incredulously stared up at my Halifax which was still circuiting at a low height.

I hurried back to the control Tower to hear the R/T conversation between the pilot and the controller. The pilot was reporting colossal vibration (little wonder, since all his airscrews were unbalanced having had eight inches ripped off the blades!) and difficulty in climbing and he was asking for instructions as he had a full bomb-load on board.

Wing Commander Young remained calm and had sized up the situation after hearing of what we had found at the end of the runway. He instructed the pilot to jettison his bombs off the coast at Bridlington, then to fly inland, turn back towards the sea, set the automatic pilot on an easterly course and bale out the crew. This was a wise decision for a belly landing would have been hazardous in view of the power needed to keep the Halifax even airborne. It was now 2.30 a.m. and the pilot, who was unsure of the extent of damage to his aircraft, obeyed the instructions and finally baled out his crew, who landed safely around the Yorkshire Wolds. The Halifax we presumed droned on across the North Sea with 'George' at the controls until it ran out of petrol and crashed into the sea.

Bomber Command now had a brainwave. They decided that a daylight raid on Germany would be possible if there was broken cloud all the way to the target, their theory being that the Halifax could hop from cloud to cloud and that way dodge the fighters. The Squadron Commander picked me and Pete Warner for this experiment, on instructions from Bomber Harris to our AOC and we were duly told to stand by. Pete was a great friend of mine; he had the nicest personality – I was very fond of him and we later had lots of fun together. (He was tragically shot down by one of our own Mosquitos in Egypt.) Pete and I couldn't believe that anyone could be so stupid as to go through with this farce. I couldn't sleep at night from sheer terror and I hastily wrote a letter saying goodbye to my mother which I sealed and handed to the Station Padre ('Holey Coley').

The next morning we were warned to stand up for a 2 p.m. take-off for Essen in the Ruhr. I was absolutely petrified, couldn't eat lunch and when I looked at Peter Warner his face expressed my own feelings. We were to die in roughly three hours. Our only hope was a Mosquito Photographic Reconnaissance which was in process of going over our route to establish the amount of cloud – we were to await his return before any decision was made. We sat like condemned men waiting the electric chair and a quarter of an hour seemed an eternity. We attended a briefing, just the two of us.

Everyone was most sympathetic but so far no news.

At the eleventh hour the Mosquito returned with the information that there was no cloud after the Dutch coast so our operation was cancelled for the day. We never heard anything more about this scatterbrained plan and I can only assume that Wing Commander Young must have convinced Group Headquarters of the impossibility of the task. I felt honoured to have been picked with Pete Warner out of the whole of Command but I was more than grateful at our reprieve. I promptly went and ate a huge lunch and so did Pete Warner. Afterwards we played table tennis to release our pent-up feelings.

During early March we heard a rumour that we were to attack the German battleship *Tirpitz*, which was lying heavily camouflaged at Aasen Fjord near Trondheim. The plan was for two squadrons to attack the *Tirpitz;* one squadron (ours) was to drop 4,000 lb bombs to try and put off the gunners and the shore batteries and the other squadron was to go in at mast height with mines. The idea was to fly straight at the ship beamwards and drop the mines against the side of the mountain. They would then roll down the slope and lodge between the *Tirpitz* and the mountain and explode. This would ensure a beautifully restricted explosion which would blow in the steel panels of the ship! I'd never heard such rubbish and imagined some young statistician at Bomber Command sitting down and working out this insane plan. Nevertheless it was carried out.

On 27th March we were ordered to fly to the advanced base at Kinloss where I had done my Whitley course. That afternoon a Mosquito landed at Kinloss with photos of the exact position of the *Tirpitz*, together with a close-up of the latest camouflage. These photos had been taken by a Norwegian patriot at the risk of his life and rushed to Sweden where a Mosquito was standing by to fly the film to Northern Scotland. Such was the excellence of our Intelligence Service. The weather report was good, with slight sea fog at the target, so we were briefed, bombed up and fed. The Halifax was not really the ideal aircraft to carry a 4,000 lb bomb because it was about the size of a pillar box and the bomb doors wouldn't quite close. This meant that there was a good deal of air resistance which slowed down the speed of the aeroplane. With a 4,000 lb bomb on board we couldn't take a full petrol load either. Consequently the operation to Trondheim was stretching our endurance to some-thing like twenty minutes flying in hand.

We took off about 10 p.m. in failing light, and set course for Norway, which meant about four hours flying across the North Sea. We saw with relief about four destroyers 25, 50, 75 and 100 miles from base in a line to Norway, and realised that they were there for our benefit on return, in case anyone ran short of petrol. Whilst the North Sea crossing was tedious at least we had no flak or fighters, and all one needed to dwell on was the forthcoming reception at Trondheim! We crossed the Norwegian coast and the scenery looked marvellous from the air since it was never really dark.

We then saw the most colossal barrage ahead from the *Tirpitz* and it seemed as if every gun in Norway had been moved to Aasen Fjord. We were at 4,000 feet and at this height there was a very slight risk that we might be hit by our own bomb fragments or at any rate we could feel the blast. We started our bombing run and we could see clearly the other squadron going in at mast height. I saw a Halifax clearly below us start its run in and 300 yards from the *Tirpitz* it caught fire and exploded on the hillside.

We could see the *Tirpitz* faintly in the light from the blaze and Tim started to ask me to hold a steady course. It was not fear that prevented me, it was the sheer intensity of the flak – I just couldn't hold the Halifax steady and listened to the flak punching holes in us. The first bombing run was hopeless because the Hun had started a smokescreen, the *Tirpitz* had now disappeared under the smoke but we knew near enough where she lay and I attempted to hold the Halifax steady for a moment, imploring Tim to drop the bomb. Tim's temper was raised and he said: 'I haven't come all this bloody way to drop the bomb haphazard – you hold a steady course and I'll let it go.'

Round I went for a third bombing run, frightened to death and not at all anxious to be shot down over the snow-covered mountain. Tim said: 'Hold her steady at that' but the flak was murderous and I could hear chunks of it hitting the Halifax again. Just then I saw another low level Halifax hit and burn and crash in the valley below – a flaming torch disintegrating as it ploughed its way on its belly. Little did I know then that it was none other than Wing Commander Don Bennett, the commander of the low-level squadron, later to become Air-Vice Marshal Don Bennett in charge of the Pathfinder Group. (Later I learned from Don Bennett that he had been severely hit by the *Tirpitz* on the port wing and had burst into flames instantly. He flew straight on and belly-landed on an ice covered fjord, which accounted for my grandstand view of the aircraft disintegrating. They all got out safely, except that the wireless operator had a broken leg, and contacted a Norwegian woodsman who hid them and later escorted them over the border into Sweden. They were then interned but Bennett, being Bennett, got himself back in the bomb bay of a Mosquito some weeks later.)

Still I couldn't fly a steady course and again Tim refused to let the bomb go, so round I went for a fourth time. I said to Tim: 'I have only petrol for one more run so it's got to go this time.' I tried to hold the Halifax steady but the flak was just as severe as before and I knew I had to risk being shot out of the air to give Tim his chance. I did hold her steady for twenty seconds which seemed like twenty years, and I whooped for joy as I felt the shock of the bomb released. Tim seemed fairly confident that we dropped our bomb in the centre of the smoke screen but all I was concerned with was getting out of that bloody inferno, and quickly!

Tim Collins seemed to me to be quite fearless (I never felt I could ask him his true feelings, although we were very close) and the way he calmly bombed the *Tirpitz* with light flak being pumped straight up at him from the ground was nothing short of coolheadedness and unconcern at danger. How sad that so fine a man should die. After our first tour of operations he put in a recommendation to Bomber Command for a different plan and execution of bomber operations which was both logical and brilliant in conception. Needless to say, Bomber Command regarded a humble pilot officer's ideas as illogical and impertinent but he had an honours degree at Oxford and was no fool at the age of twenty-eight! He died before he had the chance to prove his theory.

We set course for home and I began to work out with the flight engineer just how much petrol we had left. A quick calculation told us that we had about enough to make the coast of Scotland! I immediately throttled back and set the revs as low as I could so that we should use less fuel and we began a long haul back across the North Sea. (I began to bless those destroyers that we'd seen on the way out). We crossed the Scottish coast with all the petrol tanks showing zero and I put down at the first aerodrome I saw – Lossiemouth. At de-briefing we learned that out of a bomber force of twenty-four, seven were missing and three others were down in the sea, so that attack had been very costly, both in aircraft and crews. On the credit side we later learned that the *Tirpitz* was badly damaged, but unfortunately we hadn't put her out of action as she was soon repaired and seaworthy again.

Amongst the aircraft shot down was our 'B' Flight Commander, so Hank Iveson was made a squadron leader. I was shot straight from pilot officer to flight lieutenant and appointed deputy flight commander. This was quite a jump for me, considering I'd only been commissioned three months, but life was like that and promotion in war was largely a case of filling dead men's shoes. It was also a question of experience and I was one of the few survivors with seventeen operations to my credit. The fact that I was only twenty-one didn't seem to matter very much.

We returned from advanced base on 6th April. It was good to be back at Middleton St George and in one's own bed again. On 8th April my name once again went up on the ops board and the target was Hamburg – a heavily defended port. In Hamburg is a huge lake which made finding the city an easy matter, so, typically of the Germans, they covered the whole lake with camouflage! Our bombload was two 4,000 lb bombs and again it meant going with the bomb doors slightly open. We had a fairly easy trip past the Dutch coast, from which point we could easily see Hamburg and its flak barrage and searchlight concentration; the night was clear starlight but cold at our height of 16,500 feet.

We didn't see any night fighters on this trip and bombed very accurately. The heavy flak was most unhealthy and we were hit in the port wing and fuselage over the target. I could feel the lurch as both our 4,000 lb bombs were let go but it was difficult for anyone but the bomb-aimer to see where they fell. From my seat I could only see the outskirts of the town and not much of the incendiary fires underneath me, but I had other things to think about – getting clear of the target area was one. I let Sergeant West fly the aeroplane back, even to crossing the Dutch coast and the defences, and it was good experience for him.

The next day I was called to Group Captain Traill's office and I wondered what I had done wrong. He introduced me to a gentleman named Air Commodore Hoskinson who was completely blind. (He was blinded at his front door watching a London air raid.) Hoskinson had concocted the filling for a special 8,000 lb bomb and he asked me if I was prepared to take it to Essen for him and watch the explosion. If Essen was cloud covered I was to take the bomb to Duisberg but on no account was I to drop the bomb unless I could definitely see the explosion.

This was the first 8,000 lb bomb ever to be dropped over Germany and I felt highly honoured to be the one pilot in Bomber Command picked for the job. 10th April was the night picked for me. I attended briefing in the normal way and rehearsed all the instructions given in Traill's office. I went out to my Halifax to see this huge bomb strung up in the bomb bay and it was frighteningly big! It resembled two pillar boxes stuck together, so of course, the bomb doors were fully open and I didn't relish taking off at all.

The time drew near for take-off and I began to have qualms about the ability to get the Halifax into the air, and sure enough when I got the green Aldis lamp from the control tower and I started to trundle down the main runway I realised I was over-loaded. I used the emergency boost (two minutes only at Maximum revs) and used the whole 2,000 yards of the runway before I hauled the Halifax in the air and then I was only clinging by my airscrews to the night air. Once I'd climbed up to 1,000 feet I shut off the emergency boost and to my horror I couldn't maintain height. I was really scared now and had to use the emergency boost again for about an hour to get up to a miserable 8,000 feet – I thought the engines were about to seize up and I knew that they couldn't stand very much more thrashing. I crossed the enemy coast at 8,000 feet still desperately trying to gain height but by now I had used so much fuel and was that much lighter, that I began, very slowly, to climb again.

What if a night fighter chased us? I had promised not to jettison the bomb but I had my doubts whether I could stand up to attack in my pregnant condition. As we approached Essen I had staggered up to 11,000 feet and that was as high as I could go, so we immediately got coned in searchlights and came under very heavy fire not only from heavy flak but from the light flak as well. Tim told me it was only half-clouded sky and that he could see Essen quite clearly, so we began our bombing run. I was having to fly by instruments because I was blinded by thirty odd searchlights on us – the noise and shock of the flak barrage was intense.

I remember copying David Young's technique of lowering the seat and flying on instruments but even so I couldn't resist the temptation to look out occasionally. The searchlights were terribly blinding so it really served no purpose, but when the port inner engine caught fire after a close shell burst, I watched the flames slowly extinguished and prayed silently that we would come through alive. I was not a particularly religious person – compulsory church parades and seven years at boarding school with church every Sunday had done more harm than good. Looking back over the war years, I prayed a lot to God, but I regret they were self-centred prayers for my own life and that of my wife and son! Later as a young squadron commander at North Creake, I always used to pray before an operation that I would come through safely and uninjured – and it certainly helped me to fight the fears that were constantly lurking. I must have whispered the Lord's Prayer a hundred times a year to myself!

Tim shouted, 'Bomb gone' and my old Halifax reared in the air like a horse without a jockey. Tim followed the bomb down for several thousand feet in the glare of searchlights, and when it went off there was a tremendous orange flame in the town. That was fine, but meanwhile I was in God-awful trouble and there were now about forty searchlights on us as well as intense flak. Suddenly the port inner engine was badly hit and caught fire and I gave the order to bale out as I pressed the Graviner fire extinguisher. Thank God, it worked like a charm and as I feathered the airscrew the fire gradually died out. I then heard a voice on the intercom saying, 'I've been hit'. It turned out to be the mid-upper gunner who had a large lump of shrapnel in his thigh and was bleeding like a stuck pig, poor chap.

All the interior lights had fused from flak damage and I ordered the wireless operator to give him a shot of morphia from the first aid kit, but this turned out be a very complicated business. To get him out of the turret and to cut away his Sidcot flying suit in pitch darkness was not easy and in the end I had to send Tim back with a torch to give a hand. Although it seems funny now, the poor gunner was in agony and the wireless operator shot the morphia into his thumb by mistake – his fingers being numb with cold after taking off his fleece-lined gauntlets!

Eventually someone got the morphia into him and all was well after a tourniquet had been fitted to his thigh. He never lost consciousness throughout his ordeal although he bled profusely and his calm, cool voice saying over the intercom saying 'I've been hit' impressed me. He had, of course, no idea of his injuries and the bitter cold, numbness and excitement had to some extent dulled the pain. When we got down to a lower altitude his circulation improved and he was in great pain but he never complained once. None of us really knew his thigh had been ripped open to the extent it had.

I knew many aircrew who suffered terrible injuries but felt no excruciating pain at the time, either through numbness or emotional stress. Some wonderful first-aid patching up of wounds took place in darkened bombers under the most difficult conditions and men survived who would otherwise have perished. Many pilots passed out from excessive haemorrhage after being hit and other crew members took over the controls and, with the help of ground controllers and calm advice, brought their aeroplane down in one piece. I recall one pilot being hit in the chest by a cannon shell from a Hun nighter fighter and he sat in his seat dead at the controls. I could imagine the feelings of the other members of the crew having to lift him away from the controls so that someone else could take over.

I also knew a pilot who was hit in the shoulder and one foot over Essen, but stayed at the controls in agony (and obviously terrified) and eventually landed back at base before collapsing over the controls halfway down the runway; with sheer determination and guts he defied pain and unconsciousness until he had brought his crew back safely to base.

I gave the order for an R/T message to be sent to Docking aerodrome calling for an ambulance to be available on landing and we set course with all possible speed for the Norfolk coast. I lost height rapidly and was now on three engines but weaved my way violently through the enemy defences in Holland. My mouth had gone dry from sheer terror and I felt a bit excited and shaky, but nevertheless had control of myself and of the situation. We landed at Docking and the ambulance met us at the end of the runway and took off the injured gunner. I had to spend a day there while a new engine was fitted to the port inner and I went to see my gunner in hospital at Newmarket. They had operated on his thigh and had removed a piece of shrapnel four inches long with jagged edges, as well as a half-crown and two pennies! He didn't lose his leg, but, poor man, he died some months later when he joined another crew! Such was life!

We attended de-briefing at Docking and the Intelligence officer was very piqued that we wouldn't tell him anything about the purpose of our operation, but I had been sworn to secrecy by Group Captain Traill and Air Commodore Hoskinson. Late that afternoon I took off for Middleton St George, and when we looked at the Halifax in daylight we found seventy-nine holes, including one just above the elevator control cable. There's no doubt that we were extremely lucky not to have been shot down, since it was also found necessary to change the three remaining engines for new ones. They had all nearly seized up.

Traill and Hoskinson were eager as beavers to hear the full story and Hoskinson made copious notes on the colour of the explosion and the way the bomb fell. He then asked me if I would take another one that night and I said I would if he ordered me, but I pointed out that with his bomb on board the Halifax looked and flew like a pregnant duck and I wasn't at all that keen if it meant pushing the engines to maximum boost. I admired Hoskinson and the way he wrote notes, considering that he was absolutely blind. They were both very kind to me and most concerned at what we'd all been through. I must admit that I'd been very frightened, and I look back on that trip with a shudder at what might have happened.

We were never alone on our night operations to Germany: we had always one dark-suited companion whose name was Death.

This gentle phantom might be the guide to a night fighter attack ahead, pointing to us as prey; or tired of her drab costume she might startle the night in a blaze of sequins, each one a pellet of destruction. But perhaps she was most sinister when we never saw her and could merely report death by 'aircraft failure', by collision, by bombs falling from an aircraft overhead or even death by serious pilot or crew error. She was there, always there, trimmed and manicured and with a heart of stone. She was the enemy we never conquered, the lady with no name and no features, save a cold, white smile.

The 'black widow' had long white lethal fingers: the first was the groaning lift of a bomber pregnant with steel and petrol; then the thin ribbon of the Channel, then the hostile mainland with white farmhouses and tidy villages where men and women slept between warm, clean sheets. For us only a black question mark – would we return? Would the widow carry a cold wreath to our crew's last resting place on some green Yorkshire hillside. For it was the widow who dealt the cards, spun the wheel, directed our navigation into hell or high water. She held aces, trumps, court cards, all. She was beyond escaping, always there and I would gladly lay the first stone at her tomb and trophy.

Perhaps what cut most keenly was the edge of loneliness and the wide acres of night sky; no traffic, no company, no light save an odd POW camp. Then the return, the Black Forest, interminable, the sight of England grey and sleepy. Butterflies as we made for the aerodrome and wondered if a sneaky night fighter had trailed our aircraft to destroy us almost on our own front door. The widow's smile then cracked into echoing laughter.

St John in the New Testament (Chapter IV) says that the opposite of fear is love; not bravery as one might imagine. I feel he is right. In *The Last Thing at Night*[1], the author says:

> Is the man who kneels afraid? In a sense he is. He doesn't show the symptoms of ordinary fear, a sweating brow, a panting heart. But there is a kind of fear. Perhaps you do. It isn't like the fear when a lorry nearly runs you down. Our English language has a word for this mysterious fear, the word 'AWE'. It possesses us in the presence of the unknown or the tremendous.

He also says: 'Fear is the source of bad temper, some turmoil deep in the heart of parents.'

I can't say that I entirely agree with him on this point but we have discussed this word 'fear' far into the night and it is virtually

[1] By Hugh Lavery. Tyne Tees TV, 1963.

indefinable in general terms. My friend Hugh Lavery says that fear will usually turn into hate and this, I think, is true. For we usually fear the boss so much that in the end, we hate him!

He has defined another sort of fear for me with these words: 'Fear is when man can't assign a cause to an effect.' Take, for example, a sudden nausea or faintness, a sudden rash on one's face – one is immediately and instinctively afraid because one cannot connect a cause to the effect. Think, for example, of seeing a building suddenly collapse – fearful, yet, if we are warned beforehand that this building is to be demolished we are ready for it and the explosion provokes no fear.

So 'fear' and 'awe', the latter was a common experience among bomber crews – the awesome sight of the searchlight and flak barrage at the entrance to the Ruhr; not really fear until one was enmeshed but up till then, awe. It was awe when I watched a bomber spiral down in a searchlight cone and finally explode and disintegrate into a shower of falling, incandescent fragments. Yet this same fear could often turn into a sort of sheer schoolboy excitement, a tingling thrill even in the face of violent and sudden death. Although one's chance of survival as a bomber crew was very small this fear became an incentive to survival and the instinct of self-preservation, an incentive to flying skill when attacked by a night fighter, to cunning in dodging the searchlight beams and to strict discipline and teamwork as a bomber crew. Each member had a vital part to play and his fears were submerged in the excitement of watching his pilot and captain shepherd the bomber through the defences.

There followed a fairly slack period, and after the last trip on 10th April we were constantly stood down until the end of the month when Intelligence informed Bomber Command that the *Tirpitz* had now been repaired and was ready to put to sea. Off we went again to Scotland, and flew to an advanced base at Tain near Invergordon. The tendency for ground fog at Aasen Fjord persisted and we were just aimlessly amusing ourselves until the night came for perfect conditions. This happened on 27th April, and once again we set out for Norway, only this time with a 4,000 lb bomb and four 250 lb bombs. The extra weight could be taken because since our last trip

Michael Renaut with the unflappable Professor Tim Collins.

The wedding of Michael and Yvonne Renaut. Congratulations from Air Vice-Marshal Carr.

to Norway the Merlin engines on the Halifax had been improved. When we arrived over the target a sea mist had rolled in and the *Tirpitz* wasn't visible but its gunfire gave away its position. How I loathed the ground defences at Aasen Fjord – they were vicious. The Hun obviously didn't intend the *Tirpitz* to be sunk without putting up a stout defence. Tim Collins made me do three bombing runs but we missed and he saw our stick of bombs fall harmlessly alongside the ship. No one else had any better luck so the operation was laid on again the following night. That awful grind across the North Sea was boring as hell, but at least we were safe from night fighters because in North Norway aerodromes were few and far between. Not only that, we weren't being shot at all the way there and back and this made it less of a frightening trip. This time Tim bombed well and he swears that we hit the ship under its smokescreen, but it was difficult to be sure.

Intelligence later told us that the *Tirpitz* was heavily damaged and wouldn't put to sea again for many weeks. This was some consolation for our raids, but we paid heavily in both men and aircraft.

I remember when we were stood down for a day from operating, David Young, Bill Kofoed, (a brave New Zealander) Pete Warner and I all piled into a Humber Shooting wagon at Tain and drove up to the north-west of Scotland as far as Inverkirkaig. I had bought a Remington .22 rifle in Tain and had it in the car with me, when David suddenly spotted three deer about a hundred yards from the road. He stopped the car and I took aim at the largest and let fly. In an instant David and Bill leapt out of the car, jumped a four foot fence and ran to pick up the deer while I stayed in the car pondering the frightful bit of poaching I had done! David, who was about 6 feet 2 ins tall and strong as an ox, picked up the deer, which weighed about 75 lbs, slung it across his shoulders and sprinted back to the car. It was quickly slung in the back and we drove off in a hurry. We subsequently strapped the deer across the rear turret of our Halifax and flew it back to Middleton St George, where the officers' mess had vension on the menu. I still look back and think how lucky we were not to be caught.

On return to base we had a good ENSA show and I suddenly fell heavily for one of the dancers! Being in love was a new emotion for me and I rather liked it. Hazel was a terribly attractive girl with an hourglass figure and I fell for her completely. I asked her where she was appearing next and she told me West Hartlepool, so I said I'd get there by hook or by crook. God, what a place! How anyone could bear to live there was a mystery to me, but I was in love and didn't care. Hazel used to come out with me in between shows and of course, I never missed a performance. Later she went to Northallerton and I followed her there feeling like a million dollars – not caring about flying or Middleton St George. I got so late one night that I missed the last bus and train to Darlington, and was forced to set out and walk the twenty miles home. I tried hitch-hiking but without success – no one liked stopping at one o'clock in the morning to pick up a lone airmen – I eventually reached a level crossing and the keeper, a Yorkshireman, shouted down to me: 'Would you like a cup o' tea?' So I went up into his cabin and drank a hot cup of tea and he asked me where I was bound for. When I told him Darlington he said: 'Well, that's easy. I'll close the gates to the traffic and you can nip down and ask if anyone's going to Darlington!' It worked like a charm and the second vehicle to stop, a lorry, took me right past the aerodrome gates. I liked that Yorkshire-man's cheek in closing the level crossing to traffic! Every vehicle had to stop while I nipped down to ask them where they were heading for and when I gave the signalman the 'thumbs up' he opened the gates and we were off.

Eventually Hazel left the district and I soon forgot her – we had so much excitement and fear in life that one never struck up anything too long for it was dangerous and the job we were doing needed 100 per cent concentration. We had our mad parties, our bouts of getting sloshed, our practical jokes, but these were all short-lived and life was too precious to get too involved.

I was now suffering (though I didn't know it then) from a disease called the 'Twenties' – a state of mind that came on after one had completed twenty-one operations. Nearly all our casualties occurred between twenty and thirty ops and the main reason was that pilots started to get over-careful. Instead of going through a searchlight belt or a flak barrage one tended to go round them. Fear played a large part in this: when one knew that the casualty rate was at its highest around twenty-six to twenty-eight ops it was hard not to dwell upon it in one's slacker moments. I had cut twenty-one notches on my locker door and each time I cut a fresh one I wondered if it would be the last.

On 3rd May we attacked Hamburg again but this time with a 4,000 lb bomb and four 250 lb cans of incendiaries. The town was burning well when we arrived and we came in for the usual greeting when we began our bombing run. Who was it who said, 'The natives were unfriendly'? They certainly were, and chucked all the iron at us that they could lay their hands on. Tim was undismayed. He always remained the essence of coolheadedness in an emergency. Was he as frightened as I was? I shall never know. Neither of us ever showed fear, but that didn't mean to say the emotion wasn't permanently present.

The flak on the edge of Hamburg subsided and we knew that meant night fighter interference. We all kept a sharp look out, except old Tim, who was intent on his Sperry bombsight and asking to fly a straight course. I held her beautifully steady for him to bomb and there was only desultory shelling around us. Over on our port side a Lancaster was coned badly in searchlights and must have received a direct hit in the bomb bay, or it may have been cannon fire from a fighter. Anyway, whatever it was caused a sudden explosion in the sky and flaming pieces dropped like a Roman candle to the ground. Thank God, I thought, that the seven men on board will not have felt anything. Death will have been swift and unfelt.

As we left the target area my rear gunner spotted a Messerschmitt 110 a thousand yards behind us and I told him to keep a sharp watch. The fighter had seen us and prepared to line us up in his sights but I wasn't having any. Just as he opened fire with cannon I yawed violently to port and saw his shells go winging past us on the port side. This was a trick that Cheshire had taught me and it was very effective. To yaw an aeroplane all one did was to kick hard on port or starboard rudder without allowing aileron and the effect would be for the aeroplane to crab sideways with the nose pointing either left or right. If a night fighter pilot was fooled by this manoeuvre, as he generally was, he would guess that we were about to turn to port or starboard and would deflect his fire accordingly. This greenhorn in the Messerschmitt 110 was fooled and by the time he'd realised his error I was split-arsing all over the sky and he never saw us again!

We spotted two Messerschmitt 109's on our starboard beam but they were intent on some other poor victim and never saw us. Tim Collins was somewhat alarmed by my erratic manoeuvres and he accused me of upsetting his navigation calculations, but I told him in no uncertain terms that if a fighter was on our tail I was going to gyrate all over the sky and he'd have to pick up the threads of navigation after we'd shaken him off. Home we went across sleepy Holland and back to bed – and operation number 22 was duly notched up on my cupboard door with some trepidation.

I had now great faith in the Halifax and its handling qualities and I had seen how it stood up to a battering. Mind you, it took strength in the forearms and wrists to hurl it about the sky, and unlike the Lancaster it responded slowly and heavily. As I've said before the Lancaster was much gentler to fly but give me the Halifax for a battering every time.

Two days later we were off again, this time to Stuttgart, and I had an eerie feeling that this was to be my last trip. I certainly never suffered from presentiments before but there was something about this trip which was worrying me. We took off and carried out our normal climb to altitude and as I left the English Channel coast we were at 16,000 feet. I crossed the enemy coast at Dunkirk when suddenly there was a frightful scream from the port out engine. I had a quick look at the instruments and the port outer revs had gone off the clock! This meant that the reduction gear on the airscrew had gone for a burton and the engine would have seized up had I not immediately feathered.

This didn't stop the airscrew windmilling though and I had to make a quick decision. After a short conference with Tim I decided to return to base, as to undertake such a deep penetration on three engines would have been unwise if not madness. We got two pastings over Dunkirk, one coming and the other going, but this was vastly preferable to a long and dangerous trip to Stuttgart. Funny that I should have had eerie feelings over this trip! Perhaps God himself stepped in and prevented the operation being completed – I do not know.

On 14th May rumours got about that Bomber Harris was to

launch an attack on Germany with 1,000 bombers and we were told
to stand by for a 'Maximum Effort'. The secret, which really was
Top Secret, had leaked out despite the strict security. Everyone
seemed to know and great excitement prevailed. Nobody knew the
target but everyone was alerted, the training groups as well as the
operational squadrons, and we did nothing but air-test our
machines each day in readiness. The great day dawned on 30th May
and at briefing the target was announced as Cologne. Conditions,
we were told by the meteorological officer, would be superb. A clear
cloudless night with a full moon. What better? Every single
aeroplane in our squadron was operating that night, and throughout the whole country they raised 1,053 aircraft of assorted shapes,
types and sizes. We took off at about 10 p.m. – the final wave to
bomb – and I could simply not believe my eyes at the Dutch coast at
what I saw 100 miles ahead of us. It was a gigantic fire that an hour
before had been the city of Cologne. There it was on fire from end to
end, with still another 300 bombers to deliver their load.

I had never seen anything of the London blitz and had never
been in London during an air-raid so I always imagined the
Germans were suffering more than we were in Britain. I was in
Devon throughout the worst period of the Battle of Britain and the
blitz that followed so I knew nothing of the misery and suffering of
Londoners. Being a true 'cockney' myself, I felt for them later when
I knew more of their ordeal, which they withstood like heroes. (I
would far rather have faced death in a bomber than to have sat
huddled in an air-raid shelter being bombed!) Later on in 1944 and
1945 the German civil population suffered worse than anyone and,
make no mistake, they deserved what was coming to them. They
were on the receiving end of such things as ten-ton bombs and
4,000 lb phosphorus bombs – the latter could set whole streets
alight and burn people alive in thick concrete air-raid shelters. The
12,000 and 20,000 lb armour piercing bombs would penetrate the
deep shelters and tube stations underground in Berlin with
tremendous effect on the civilians, who thought they were safe in
Potsdamer Platz tube station. In fact 650 people died after a 12,000
lb bomb had penetrated 100 feet underground! Londoners had a
ghastly time but at least they were safe on the underground station
platforms.

Tim Collins had no need to navigate – there was our target ahead of us and we went like moths to a candle! I saw dozens of strange aeroplanes in the moonlit sky – Wellingtons, Hudsons, Whitleys, Hampdens, Halifaxes, Manchesters, Ansons, Lancasters and Oxfords all making their way to the blaze ahead. We arrived over Cologne at our appointed time and the defences were swamped – just the occasional bit of flak and a handful of searchlights – but there were hundreds of night fighters about and they were taking their toll. I believe I'm right in saying that 1,016 bombers actually reached Cologne out of the 1,053 sent out. We placed our bombs and incendiaries in that part of the town that wasn't already alight – an easy job for Tim at last and he made the most of his opportunity. The trip was absolutely uneventful but we saw a number of night fighter combats all around us and the defences were still flinging flak about. We were lucky and were not attacked, and we landed back at base after 5 hours and 40 minutes in the air. There was a buzz of conversation in the locker room and crews were saying what a raid it had been. Photographic Reconnaissance aircraft went to Cologne the next day and photographed the city. Approximately 60 per cent of the city had been set alight and the homeless must have numbered thousands.

It was a feather in Bomber Harris's cap and marked the turning point of Bomber Command's part in the war. Unfortunately he made the mistake of immediately attacking another city in conditions of cloud and poor visibility and the effects were puny compared to the damage on Cologne.

Why he couldn't wait for ideal meteorological conditions I'll never know, but the fact remains that Essen and Bremen were attacked by a force of over a thousand bombers whilst there was low cloud and poor visibility and the confidence that the High Command had obtained through Cologne was dissipated. A few months later 1,000 bombers in a night operation were commonplace, but Bomber Command very nearly didn't make the grade as a weapon of war.

Anyway, two nights after Cologne raid, we set out, 1,036 strong, to attack Essen, but as we approached the Ruhr we could see thin cloud and industrial haze all over the target and environs. The fires were scattered and widespread, but the defences were concentrated and accurate and we ourselves came under heavy fire on our bombing run. The Ruhr always put up a good defence and we were never really happy in the 'Happy Valley' as it was called. Just on the edge of the Ruhr was a town called Munchen-Gladbach to which we always gave a wide berth. Intelligence told us that this was the place where budding gunners were trained in the art of shooting down bombers and quite obviously if one inadvertently flew near enough, there were several instructors ready to show their prowess to beginners.

Tim Collins had a simple task in bombing the existing fires but we were not sure exactly where Essen lay under the low cloud. Pathfinder, Target Market and Master Bomber techniques were unknown until late 1943 and of course, they increased the efficiency of Bomber Command operations enormously. Until then the value of Bomber Command raids were doubtful, even to the effect on morale of the German civilian population of 1,000 Bomber raids, but the formation of the No 8 Pathfinder Bomber Group under the command of Air Vice-Marshal D.C.T. Bennett and later the brilliant, courageous, low level target marking techniques of Group Captain G.L. Cheshire, vc, transformed Bomber Command into a powerful and effective force.

Here again, I think it was as a result of Cheshire's daring low level flights over Germany by night on his first tour of operations, that convinced him that low level marking by night was comparatively safe and effective. To hit a fast flying Mosquito at night at low level (50 to 100 feet) was a difficult task and Chesh got away with it scores of times. I think he would agree that our sympathies lay with the Master Bombers! These were pilots who had often done two tours of operations and yet still volunteered to circle a heavily defended target like Berlin or Essen for an hour or more, directing, by cool verbal instruction over the R/T, where the main force should aim their bombs. Since our coloured target markers were immediately duplicated by the Germans some five or ten miles from the target itself and bomber crews were naturally fooled by such ruses, in order not to waste effort, bombs and lives and to prevent dummy targets being attacked, the Master Bomber simply told the 800 odd bomb aimers exactly what to do and which markers to bomb. Even PFF made mistakes and markers were wrongly placed on occasions, but again the Master Bomber told the crews to ignore the markers and bomb under his orders.

It was no wonder that incredibly brave men like Wing Commander Guy Gibson, VC of the Dambuster Squadron, lost their lives as Master Bombers. We were lucky, on average, in being in the target area for three minutes only, whereas the Master Bomber was being shot at non-stop for a period of half to one hour! What cool courage.

We dropped our bombs and got clear of the Ruhr in a hurry, picking our way through the searchlight concentrations. Again we saw no night fighters and I counted myself lucky that the operation had gone according to plan. Something like forty bombers were lost over Essen, which was more than were lost over Cologne, but then, the defences were far greater over the Ruhr.

The Command was dissatisfied with the result of the operation on Essen, so we were briefed on 8th June to go again. I was standing on the perimeter track near the take-off runway at about 11 p.m. when suddenly I heard the word 'Sir' over the intercom and who should walk in and sit beside me in full flying kit but Group Captain Traill, our Station Commander. He politely informed me that he was taking the place of my second pilot and coming with us to Essen. I was flabbergasted at this though I felt very honoured to have my Station Commander as a passenger. It was also very brave of Group Captain Traill because as a Station Commander he was not supposed to fly operationally and could have kept his safe seat at Middleton St George if he'd wished. However, strictly against regulations, he had decided to do an operation.

I was terribly apprehensive at carrying such important 'cargo'. He put us all at our ease immediately and asked me to be captain of the aircraft and to treat him like an ordinary member of the crew. This was all very well! We had an uneventful trip as far as the Dutch coast but things began to hot up after that. For the first time we saw a new German weapon in the sky; it was a sort of dustbin which was shot up to about 16,000 feet full of phosphorus, magnesium, nuts and bolts, explosive, bits of iron and everything but the kitchen stove. The effect when it exploded was just like an aircraft being shot down – a colossal flash followed by a cascade of falling flaming fragments. I think the Hun meant it to look like an exploding aircraft just to unnerve us in the target area.

I showed Group Captain Traill how to evade searchlights as we ran up to the target area and explained about my weaving to avoid the heavy flak. He seemed nervous but excited and was busy looking round the night sky at the performance put on in our honour. There was still a good deal of cloud over the Ruhr and Essen was so spread about that it wasn't easy to pin-point the middle of the town. Tim Collins set me on my bombing run which I did with a silent glide approach, and we bombed reasonably satisfactorily. Just after leaving the target we suddenly saw a Ju88 on our starboard side and he shot across our bows firing his cannon and machine gun tracer at another Halifax a hundred yards on our port side. The Ju88 never saw us; he was too intent on his prey and the poor wretched Halifax suddenly burst into flames along its starboard wing.

I was fascinated with fear and watched the doomed aircraft start to spiral downwards and I thought how easily it could have been us. I think the Hun must have hit the pilot and second pilot because the aircraft immediately went into a spin down a searchlight cone and no parachutes were seen opening. Traill didn't look at all happy at that moment and I expect he was probably wondering why he'd ever come with us.

We were just leaving the Ruhr valley when the blue tinted Master searchlights started hunting for us. If the Master searchlight, which was automatically controlled, found you, the other searchlights fastened on and in a matter of seconds you could be coned badly. I was weaving fairly broadly and each time the Master searchlight moved to find us we moved against its direction and we crossed the sky. The flak was still noisy and unpleasant and there were quite a number of 'dustbins' being chucked up near the target area, but we soon got clear and set course for the Belgian coast.

The usual reception awaited us there and as soon as we were through it I instructed the wireless operator to send a message to Group Headquarters telling them that our valuable cargo was safe! I asked Traill if he wanted to fly for a bit but he declined and drank his coffee with much relief beside me. Everyone looked alike, a flying helmet and oxygen mask and all that was identifiable were their eyes – those sometimes showed their emotions but in the darkness it was hard to tell the difference between fear and joy. We landed back at base after a trip of only five hours fifty minutes and attended briefing.

On 12th June I went home on twelve days' leave and I felt I needed the rest. More particularly to be free from the fear of death for twelve days was something on its own. My parents were pleased to see me and I was asked by the local ATC to give a couple of lectures to the pupils. I went up to London to see my uncle and aunt and I told my uncle how frightful it must be to live in Germany under the colossal bombardment they were enduring. He said that London was just as bad, if not worse, and proceeded to take me on a conducted tour of the East End and the City of London. I must confess that the damage impressed me; I had never before seen such destruction. I think that car ride did me good! I went back to the squadron convinced that the raids on Germany were fully deserved and I no longer had any sympathy for the Germans.

I returned from leave refreshed and immediately saw my name on the ops board. It was to be the third (and last of the series) thousand bomber raid on Germany and the target was Bremen. At briefing we were told that the weather should be fine over the target but that there would be a good deal of cloud. Whatever happened we were ordered to bomb *below* cloud and everyone in Bomber Command was told the same thing. We took off eventually at around 10.30 p.m. on 25th June and made our way to the target – the moon was still bright and one could see hundreds of other bombers around the sky. I thought what a benefit for the Hun night fighters! The flak around Bremen was effective but there were no searchlights as the town was under 10/10th cloud.

I circled the target and Tim and I watched the bombing; we could see the bright light of fires reflected on the underside of the cloudbase – the cloud layer was thin for us to have seen this. I said to my crew: 'Well . . . here goes . . . Bremen, here we come.'

We were at 16,000 feet and I started a diving turn round the city until I was doing over 300 mph. The Halifax was shuddering violently and obviously didn't like this speed and I observed that we were still a long way from the cloudbase when we got down to 7,000 feet. I wondered what the rest of Command were doing, but I was in the midst of severe light flak being pumped up at us through the cloud. Again I thought why does Bomber Harris send over 1,000 bombers to Bremen on a cloudy night? . . . surely with a bit more patience he could have clear starlit skies.

I dithered over the decision that I had to make. Must I obey our instructions to the letter or can I justly say that we bombed at 7,000 feet because of 10/10ths cloud? I knew it would be suicidal to go beneath cloud because from where we were the cloudbase was obviously about 2,000 feet. Without consulting my crew I knew I had to make a decision and I reluctantly decided to go down. I held the fate of seven men in my hands by that decision and I began to wonder, as I started the final dive, whether it was fair of me not to put the question to them and take a majority vote. However I'd done it and if we were killed it was Bomber Command's fault, not mine.

I levelled out at 3,000 feet *still* above cloud and not one member of the crew had called me in the intercom since we started losing height from 16,000 feet. That was ominous. They all knew what I was doing and they must have been very frightened. My airspeed was not in excess of 300 mph and 'in for a penny, in for a pound' I dived down through the cloud on a fast straight bombing run and finally broke cloud over Bremen docks at 1,200 feet.

I was hurtling through the air at 325 mph and everything seemed to happen at once – Tim was shouting: 'This is marvellous, I can see everything.' I was shouting at the two gunners to blaze away at the searchlights and guncrews as it was like broad daylight with the fires reflected on the base of the cloud. The wireless operator had drawn his curtain and called out: 'God, Skipper, what a wonderful sight.' Tim was yelling: 'Hold her steady. Left, left . . . right a bit.'

We flashed across the town with light flak streaming at us from every direction and I could hear holes being punched in the Halifax. Tim suddenly shouted: 'Bombs gone. Christ, it's bloody wonderful – look at our bombs heading straight for the docks – we've hit them fair and square . . . God, this is marvellous.'

I knew we'd be shot down the next second and my hair felt as if it was pushing upwards under my helmet with fear. My mouth had gone dry and my heart was pounding through my Sidcot flying suit, but despite my fear I kept in command of my faculties. We not only felt the blast of our own bombs but we were peppered by them (later the armourers found pieces of British shrapnel in the Halifax) and immediately I heard 'Bombs gone' I hauled back on the stick and our colossal impetus and forward speed took us straight up to 10,500 feet where I levelled out. The rear gunner was telling me that the light flak was yards behind, and quite obviously the Hun gunners had underestimated our flying speed.

I climbed back up to 16,000 feet and felt utterly relieved to have got clear of that inferno without being killed. The flak at the Dutch coast was like pea-shooters after what we'd been through and I soon crossed the North Sea and made for base where we landed at 4.45 a.m. When we all went in for de-briefing the Intelligence Officer asked me what sort of trip we'd had and when I said that we'd bombed below cloud he nearly had a fit. Apparently I was the only aircraft in the whole of Bomber Command to have gone below cloud.

The Intelligence Officer said: 'What about the balloon barrage? . . . What about all the bombs falling on you from the rest of the main force?' I nearly collapsed when he mentioned balloons, for the memory of Coventry was still fresh in my mind, but to think I had flown through Bremen's balloon barrage nearly finished me off!

We had undoubtedly been very lucky to survive, and the funny thing is that Wing Commander Young immediately recommended me for the DFC! Had he known how terrified I had been and had he realised that I was only obeying the briefing orders, he might not have done so! Still it was nice to wear a DFC ribbon, however ill-gotten.

We were all so excited and so wide awake that instead of going straight to bed we hung about in the ops room and listened to other crews being debriefed. We lost five aircraft from the squadron that night (nearly six!) and I believe most of them were shot down by night fighters. The low cloud bank and the incendiary fires made bombers stand out in silhouette and the German night fighters must have had a fairly easy task in finding targets.

Looking back to those awful deep penetrations into Germany, the strain took its toll and it was a wonder to me that there weren't more cases of LMF (Lack of Moral Fibre). One had to be constantly on the alert and ever watchful for night fighters which were the real danger. It was an easy matter for the Hun; he only had to find the bomber stream or identify the target or rendezvouz and there were a thousand four-engined bombers for his picking. I believe that the record held by a Hun night fighter pilot was nine four-engined bombers in one night. Such a claim was never made in Britain for our night fighters never had the concentrations of bombers either on the way to, or over the target area.

The strain I think was aptly put by W.J. Lawrence who wrote the history of No 5 Bomber Group. He wrote:

To be a member of a bomber crew required persistent fortitude at a time and in circumstances when the stoutest mind and heart would have every excuse to show a natural and normal weakness. The average operation was in darkness and the early hours of the morning; everyone who took part in it knew that casualties were so high that the odds were against the survival of any particular airman. It never was and never could be a mode of warfare to be conducted in hot blood; the bomber crew was engaged throughout a flight in a series of intricate tasks resembling those of a skilled craftsman in his workshop; calculations and minute adjustments of machinery had to be made all the time with a clear head and a steady hand. And a long flight by night is in itself no task for a weakling when a small navigation error may result in a forced landing at the best. But all this had to be done in the face of the most formidable defences against air attack that the wit of man and a vast organisation could devise.

Searchlights and anti-aircraft guns set up a visible and terrifying barrier between the bomber and the target, but the far more deadly night fighter might at any moment during the flight of hundreds of miles over enemy territory strike without warning within a period to be counted in seconds; in all such encounters a bomber aircraft by its very nature was at a gross disadvantage with inferior speed, manoeuvrability, and fire power. No one who was present at a bomber airfield before, during and after an operation could for a moment be unconscious of the unnatural and inhuman strain to which so many young men were being subjected; until all was over no one could feel the tension relaxed or forget what was at stake.[1]

[1] *No 5 Bomber Group RAF 1939-45*, Faber & Faber, 1951.

I often heard it said that the great majority of four-engined bombers shot down never saw their attacker. Most of the highly skilled night fighter pilots closed on their prey from the blind spot below and aft and then usually only needed to fire once to hit the petrol tanks or the bombload. I spoke to a great friend of mine, Squadron Leader Lashbrook, DSO, DFC, when he escaped to Gibraltar from being shot down over Czechoslovakia, and he told me that some of his crew spotted the night fighter that got him – the first thing they knew was that the port wing suddenly burst into flames. Lashbrook gave the order to bale out and stayed at the controls whilst the six crew abandoned the aircraft, but when he went to leave himself the port wing burned off and the Halifax started to spiral viciously. The centrifugal force was terrific and it was only after using superhuman strength that he did succeed in leaving the pilot's seat and baling out. (When trying to struggle out of his seat, his harness got caught up in the undercarriage and flap levers and the Halifax fell 14,000 feet in flames before he was able to get clear and jump – he said those few frightening minutes seemed an eternity.)

On his return to UK Squadron Leader Lashbrook told me of his miraculous and quick escape to Gibraltar. He landed by parachute in a ploughed field at 2 o'clock in the morning in pitch darkness, buried his parachute and hid in some woods. By night only, he walked from Czechoslovakia, through Germany and into France, alone, before he contacted the 'Rabbit Run' escape organisation run by Colonel Patrick O'Leary (also known as Colonel Guérisse and 'Monsieur Courage'). This remarkable and efficient escape network organised by Belgian, Dutch and French agents escorted Lashbrook to the Spanish border (the Pyrenees) and enabled him to reach Lisbon in under three weeks from Czechoslovakia! It was on the sun terrace of a hotel in Lisbon that Lashbrook read in *The Times* the notice: 'Squadron Leader Lashbrook, DFC, missing believed killed!' He tried to describe to me the feelings that ran through his mind as he read that announcement – 'There but for the Grace of God, go I'! In due course he left for Gibraltar and was flown home for further duty. I believe he survived the war, but I'm not sure. He was awarded the DSO and certainly deserved to survive two tours of ops.

At the beginning of July word got around via the grapevine that the squadron was being groomed for some special work, and during the first few days we carried out petrol consumption tests. It was anybody's guess what we were being trained for but most people thought it was a special long distance flight to Russia or Africa. Security on the station was so severe that we were confined to camp for the whole of the next week and guesses got wilder, and wilder. I used to go for long walks in the evening sunshine with Lawrence Meynell (the well-known author), our adjutant, and although I pumped him in secret he never let on what he knew. Looking back I don't think Meynell knew what was afoot. He had a lovely caustic sense of humour and I used to enjoy our walks round the hedgerows.

CHAPTER IV

Middle East

On 13th July all crews were summoned to briefing and it was announced that our target was the Italian fleet, which was concentrated in the Eastern Mediterranean. We were to take off the next morning at 6 a.m. for Gibraltar, and warned, as we were only going for about seven days, not to take anything but a spongebag, a steel helmet and a suit of khaki drill in lightweight material. All this was to be arranged on the evening of 13th July and the engine fitters were busy fitting sand filters and loading spare engines in our aircraft. We were instructed to leave our rooms exactly as they were . . . not to touch any of our personal belongings as we should be back inside a week. The Station buzzed with activity and we were all very excited at the thought of Egypt and the Middle East, but security was rigid. Even our letters home were opened and censored and the outgoing 'phone lines were cut completely; finally we were asked not to write any letters for the first seven days.

At precisely six a.m. on 14th July I became airborne together with six crew, and four fitters as passengers, two spare engines and a great deal of sundry aircraft spares. Our route took us across to Blackpool, then south-west off the Welsh coast, a long haul over the Atlantic to make landfall at Cap Finisterre, down off the coast of Portugal and round into Gibraltar. All went according to plan and by the time we reached Cap Finisterre it was very hot and I started to discard clothing. At six a.m. in Yorkshire it was quite chilly and I started off in a Sidcot flying suit, woollen pullovers and battledress but by Finisterre I was left in battledress only. As we passed Lisbon the sun was beating through the Perspex canopy above my head and I discarded my battledress and later everything except my thin underpants. (I must have looked a sight!)

Our first sight of the 'Rock' was thrilling and for me who had never been further than Germany this was a tremendous experience.

The runway looked exceedingly short (it was in fact 1,200 yards) and if one overshot one went off the end into the sea. The air was very bumpy as we made our circuit and we were buffeted about by the cross winds, but on the final approach I held her on plenty of engine revs and made what was known as a powered approach and landing. I sat the Halifax down at the extreme end of the runway and never thought I'd stop rolling before the far end, but violent use of the brakes did the trick and we taxied off to dispersal.

I could see a number of other Halifaxes scattered round the aerodrome. There were two squadrons sent from Yorkshire 4 Group – ours and No 10 Squadron under the command of Wing Commander Seymour Price. We had been in the air 8¾ hours and were tired and swelteringly hot so we went in the Mess for tea. I had always heard that if one was hot it was best to drink lots of boiling hot tea but I proved this to be a fallacy! I drank eight cups and felt hotter than ever so I took everything off and plunged into the Mediterranean while the perspiration poured off me.

By six o'clock it got cool and we dressed and went into the town to explore the night life. This consisted mainly of sleazy cafes and night clubs where the drinks were expensive and potent, and one had to more or less keep one's hand on one's wallet. We were due to take off at 6 p.m. the next day for the Canal Zone in Egypt and consequently we weren't too late going to bed because of the long flight that lay ahead. The Halifaxes were loaded to their maximum capacity with fuel, and the 1,200 yards of runway looked exceedingly short; in fact there were motor launches spaced at half mile intervals off the end of the runway so that if anyone didn't make it they stood a good chance of being rescued.

Promptly at six p.m. we lined up on the runway and began our take-off run and I literally had to haul the Halifax off the ground at less than safe flying speed at the far end of the runway. I couldn't get my speed above 100 mph and flew at fifty feet for thirty-five miles before I could start to gain height. It was a very interesting flight because as it grew dark around 7 p.m. we could see for the first time towns lit up and they looked fascinating. On the port side we could Spanish towns and on the starboard side Algerian towns. After dark we were routed over Algiers and then back into the centre of the Mediterranean and we seemed to see nothing for hours until suddenly we could see gunfire and searchlights over on our port side. I asked Tim where we were and he explained that this was in all probability Malta having an air raid. It must have been, because although it was a long way away there was prolonged and heavy gunfire. After that we saw nothing but sea and the trip grew very tedious until landfall about 11½ hours from take off. This was the Nile Delta and we were tired! It looked hot and hazy even as dawn broke and we turned and few down the Suez Canal until we reached our destination, Kabrit aerodrome.

We landed exactly twelve and a quarter hours after take off and even though it was only 5.15 a.m. it was already hot and smelly. The flies abounded and kept settling on my nose and face and I longed for a fly swat . . . Wing Commander Young already had a beauty which he had brought with him and was using to good effect. I simply cannot describe the flies of Egypt – they were just undescribable! Not only were there millions of them but they would insist on settling on one's nose. <u>The English fly is much more tolerable and at least keeps himself to himself, but the Egyptian fly drives you round the bend in five minutes.</u>

We ate a scrappy breakfast of corned beef and tea made with tinned milk and at eight a.m. took off for our base which was Aqir in Palestine (as it then was). Palestine from the air looked a green, beautiful country after the endless sand of Egypt and when we landed I knew the place was just up my street. There was green grass, lovely wooded slopes of citrus groves, a cool breeze and a blue, blue sky . . . what more could we want? The mess was a wooden hut affair but very comfortable, and at the bar all one seemed to drink was fresh, iced orange juice at a piastre a pint (about 2½d.). Most of the hardened spirit drinkers of Middleton St George were converted to orange juice at once and I much preferred it to beer and whisky.

Intelligence informed us that the Italian fleet had dispersed overnight; apparently German spies at La Linea in Spain had reported two squadrons of four-engined bombers arriving at Gibraltar and had put two and two together. That left us without a target, so we reasonably thought that we'd spend a week in Palestine and Egypt and then return home. That, however, was not to be; the battle of El Alamein was not far off and High Command decided that they could usefully employ two heavy bomber squadrons in long range targets, so we stayed.

On 25th July we were ordered to an advanced base, LG224 near Cairo, and from there we were briefed for an attack on Tobruk Harbour. We were given a meal composed of corned beef, tomatoes and sweet potatoes which was revolting and to make it worse we had to eat the meal under a net. This awful palaver of putting the net over one's head and tucking it under the plate was to prevent the flies from following the food into one's mouth! Again I find it difficult to describe what foul pests the Egyptian flies were . . . they came in their thousands and settled on every bare part of one's body, particularly one's face. Eating was no easy matter and they even managed to get inside the net and into one's mouth.

We were bombed up with six 1,000 lb bombs and eight 250 lb and enough petrol to give us an hour's flying time in hand and we took off around 10 p.m. for Tobruk. Tim found the navigation easy as we simply flew along the coast road all the way to Tobruk. It was a strange sensation flying over enemy territory and not being shot at – a relaxed feeling quite unlike the apprehension of hours over German-occupied Europe. Apparently there was a handful of enemy fighters but thank God we never saw any in all our trips to Tobruk.

As we approached our target we could see the searchlights and flak barrage and it certainly looked menacing and brought back memories of Kiel and Bremen. The Hun evidently wished to protect his main supply port and he had a fierce concentration of heavy flak to welcome us. We began our bombing run and almost immediately came under heavy fire. This was most disconcerting as we had imagined that the defences would be light. Tim was guiding me to the docks and shipping and I was having a job to hold a steady course, but he eventually shouted 'Bombs gone' and I was pleased to dive and turn out of range of the guns. We were hit several times and it remained a surprise to me that we should find such opposition but it was nice and quiet all the way back to base and safety, after five hours fifty minutes in the air.

Tim and I spotted a number of lights in the desert on the way home and it appeared that some of these were Arab encampments but a number were German camps. We decided amongst ourselves that in future we would keep one 1,000 lb bomb back from our Tobruk bombload and deliver it on a German camp. I swore all the crew to secrecy and said that we'd really have some fun next time we visited Tobruk but it wasn't to be mentioned at de-briefing. Our bombing of Tobruk that night had been accurate despite the heavy opposition and I knew that with no opposition at all and a clear moonlit night we might really shake some sleepy Huns in their tents. I looked forward to this with great relish. We spent the night at LG (landing ground) 224 and flew back to Aqir the following day – advanced base was exactly 1½ hours flying time away.

The next day we drove into Tel Aviv to look around and I was very impressed with this modern city that had sprung up in the last twenty years. The population was about 60 per cent German Jewish and all the shopkeepers seemed to be German which was a great advantage to me, as I spoke fluent German at that time. I remember one occasion when I went into a shirt shop in Tel Aviv and asked the price of a shirt in English. The woman behind the counter called to her husband in German, 'There's an English RAF officer who wants to buy a shirt; what shall we charge him?' Back came the reply '2.5.0' so I said to the woman also in German 'And what have you decided to charge me?' She very nearly collapsed with shock and blushed deep scarlet, but after that we became friendly and I later played bridge with them and some of their friends at the local bridge club.

It was a fortnight before we operated again and with so much spare time and a new and fascinating country to explore, our life was very pleasant. The bathing at Tel Aviv was marvellous and we all used to foregather at the Jaffa club just outside the town and spend our day there, eating, swimming and sunbathing. Being fair-skinned I had to be very careful and whereas most of the squadron used to parade in shorts and not much else, I always wore a bush shirt and long trousers for fear of getting burnt. The heat was something I'd never experienced before and I could never really get used to it, nor the flies, which although not as abundant as in Egypt, were nevertheless pests.

We flew to advanced base again on 8th August and spent the night there preparatory to taking off for Tobruk the following evening. We again had a quiet and unmolested trip to the target but

الحكومة البريطانية **BRITISH GOVERNMENT**

الى كل عربى كريم

السلام عليكم ورحمة الله وبركاته وبعد ، فحامل هذا الكتاب ضابط بالجيش البريطاني وهو صديق
وفى لكافة الشعوب العربية فنرجو أن تعاملوه بالعطف والاكرام . وأن تحافظوا على حياته من كل
طارىء، ونأمل عند الاضطرار أن تقدموا له مايحتاج اليه من طعام وشراب . وأن ترشدوه الى
أقرب معسكر بريطاني . وسنكافئكم مالياً بسخاء على ماتسدونه اليه من خدمات .
والسلام عليكم ورحمة الله وبركاته؟
القيادة البريطانية العامة في الشرق الاوسط

To All Arab Peoples — Greetings and Peace be upon you. The bearer of this letter is an
Officer of the British Government and a friend of all Arabs. Treat him well, guard him from
harm, give him food and drink, help him to return to the nearest British soldiers and you will
be rewarded. Peace and the Mercy of God upon you. *The British High Command in the East*

SOME POINTS ON CONDUCT WHEN MEETING THE ARABS IN THE DESERT.

Remove footwear on entering their tents. Completely ignore their women. If thirsty drink
the water they offer, but DO NOT fill your waterbottle from their personal supply. Go to their
well and fetch what you want. Never neglect any puddle or other water supply for topping up
your bottle. Use the Halazone included in your Aid Box. Do not expect breakfast if you
sleep the night. Arabs will give you a mid-day or evening meal.

REMEMBER, NEVER TRY AND HURRY IN THE DESERT, SLOW AND SURE DOES IT.

A few useful words

English	Arabic		English	Arabic
English	Ingleezi		Day	Nahaar or Yom
Friend	Sa-hib, Sa-deck.		Night	Layl
Water	Moya		Half	Nuss
Food	Akl		Half a day	Nuss il Nahaar
Village	Balaad		Near	Gareeb
Tired	Ta-eban		Far	Baeed

Take me to the English and you will be rewarded.	Hud nee eind el Ingleez wa tahud Mu-ka-fa.
English Flying Officer	Za-bit Ingleezi Tye-yara
How far (how many kilos?)	Kam kilo ?
Enemy	Germani, Taliani, Siziliani

Distance and time: Remember, Slow & Sure does it

The older Arabs cannot read, write or tell the time. They measure distance by the number
of days journey. "Near" may mean 10 minutes or 10 hours. Far probably means over a days
journey. A days journey is probably about 30 miles. The younger Arabs are more accurate.
GOOD LUCK

Government instructions for RAF personnel in the Middle East.

this time the Germans had moved in many more batteries of heavy and light flak – presumably because of 4-engined bombers attacking. The flak on the bombing run was very severe and reminded us of Trondheim and the *Tirpitz* raids, but of course visibility in the desert was very different and one could see the target clearly.

We only needed to make one bombing run as visibility was so good and Tim Collins placed our load nicely along the docks and shipping. (As arranged we kept back one 1,000 bomb). The flak kept extremely hot but evidently another Halifax was attacking simultaneously because half the searchlights were concentrated on the far side of the town and a great number of the flak batteries were not firing at us. Tim saw our bombs explode on the aiming point but there was so much smoke afterwards that it was difficult to establish what damage we'd done. Immediately after leaving the target we lost height down to 1,500 feet and flew back eastwards along the coast road, keeping our eyes open for any light.

About eighty miles from Tobruk we saw some lights burning to our starboard side and went over to have a look; unfortunately these were extinguished as soon as we flew over and it was difficult without the moon to see whether it was a Hun encampment or not. We flew on along the coast road and soon saw another gathering of lights ahead . . . We could just distinguish lines of tents which was obviously an enemy encampment so I gained height to about 2,000 feet and made a slow bombing run from west to east. Tim let the bomb go at the centre of the lights and we hoped that someone spent a disturbed night below us. We flew home satisfied at what we'd done and this time landed back at Aqir direct after seven hours in the air. We kept our secret from the Intelligence officer!

There was an orange grove near the aerodrome and Pete Warner and I decided next day to investigate it. The Arab grove owner was very hospitable and said we could help ourselves to any fruit we liked, but all we wanted to do was to stroll among the trees and marvel at the quantity of fruit. The grove consisted mainly of Jaffa oranges but there were also hundreds of lemon and grapefruit trees and there must have been millions of huge oranges just waiting to be picked. The owner explained that the majority of the fruit would be pulped to make juice as Egypt would not allow the import of fruit and there was no shipping space available for any fruit to be exported to Britain. We both ate a Jaffa orange off the tree and they were marvellous – thick-skinned and fleshy and pipless and full of juice. We discovered the grove owner's weakness was whisky and we later took him two bottles of Scotch in exchange for a lorry load of oranges – we actually picked over 3,000 in about two hours and filled the back of a thirty cwt truck! We were both pleased at the terms of exchange and later flew the oranges in the bomb bay of a Halifax up to our desert aerodrome. Water was so short that the aircrews and groundcrew were glad to have some fresh fruit in the mess.

In the rest of our spare time we usually played poker and crap. I used to enjoy the poker; the Canadians and Americans in the mess made a poker game quite remunerative and I kept a diary of my winnings. Crap was fiendish and I used to marvel at the way Canadians spoke to the dice! I don't think I know of another game where winnings can be converted into losses so quickly but in a lucky spell the dice could work marvels. It was also fascinating to roll the dice on one's knees on the carpet with a ring of excited faces. In a spell of four months I won £140 but most of that came from poker where there was considerably more skill required than at crap. Nearly all of us succumbed to gastro-enteritis or gyppy tummy, as a result of eating fresh fruit and grapes which had been contaminated by flies. Wing Commander Young went one better than all of us and got dysentery! I've never see a man look so ill – he was in agony of course and looked ashen grey and the poor man spent about two weeks in bed and then a long period of convalescence. My attack of gyppy tummy came on later than most and I spent some days in bed feeling as weak as a kitten.

I later contracted sand fly fever, then jaundice and then a rare skin complaint – all of them entirely due to the dirt of Egypt and its flies. Whenever we ate grapes they had to be dipped in a solution of permaganate of potash which was supposed to kill any germs but I feel sure that most tummy complaints were a result of eating grapes on which flies had crawled in their hundreds. We all carried fly whisks but they were quite ineffectual really and only succeeded in keeping the flies on the move.

Soon after our last operation on Tobruk the squadrons were moved from Aqir to an aerodrome in the Canal Zone called Fayid.

This was a change for the worse from my point of view as it meant leaving the lush green grass of Palestine for the sand, heat and flies of Egypt. However, it did put an end to the business of flying to an advanced base every time there was an attack on Tobruk. The one saving grace about Fayid was that it was situated on the Great Bitter Lake in the Suez Canal and the bathing at the Gazira Club was superb. All our free time was spent there and the swimming was glorious. I remember sitting at tea-time and eating plates full of fresh prawns and bread and butter. Fayid was a permanent station so the mess was very comfortable and our rooms were well ventilated and cosy – we even had an open air cinema. For our nights' entertainment we used to go into the town of Ismailia, which was not far distant, in a 30 cwt truck – it boasted two clubs – the French Club and the Greek Club – and the food at both establishments was really good. And there was QAIMNS nurses and VAD nurses from the local hospital and we used to have dances at both clubs.

We had one piece of excitement at Fayid with the arrival of the first American squadron in the Middle Eastern zone. These were B26 Marauders under the command of a Colonel Garrison and were fast twin-engined medium bombers. They were to operate against short range targets at night but the first thing we all commented upon were the great exhaust flames visible during flight. We advised the Americans to damp these down by fitting exhaust shields but they were unwilling to take advice and would only learn from experience. On their first operation to a target beyond Mersa Matruh by night they lost five night fighters. Only then did they admit they were wrong and fitted exhaust shields to all their aircraft.

I was longing to fly a Marauder and Colonel Garrison kindly let me pilot one on a short 45 minute hop round Cairo. I managed fairly well and only found difficulty in the high landing speed of 140 mph which, after the comparatively low approach speed of the Halifax, seemed as though we were going to run out of runway. In point of fact the brakes were superb and we had no difficulty in stopping, but these Marauders, I was told, were dangerous aircraft and difficult to master.

On 13th August we flew again to advanced base at LG 224 and

were bombed up for the usual haul to Tobruk. We had a more or less uneventful trip and we all found it a great relief not having any opposition on the way to the target.

We were able to see the defences at Tobruk quite clearly but at a distance the concentrations of searchlights and flak looked impenetrable, whereas over the target itself there was enough room to fly through. Unfortunately at Tobruk we in Halifaxes were usually the only attackers, apart from a handful of Wellingtons, and came in for the maximum opposition because of the lack of concentration in attack. Tim again bombed very accurately and we hoped that some supply ships would be well battered or if not that there would be damage to the dock installations. We kept back our usual 1,000 lb bomb and planted it amongst some German tents on the way home.

We went again to Tobruk on 15th August and this time I had as second pilot Group Captain Turton-Jones, our Station Commander. Again I felt honoured to be taking so high a personage and I admired him for his fortitude in coming with us. We suffered badly over Tobruk and sustained serious flak damage in the starboard outer engine. I had to feather it soon after leaving the target area and a few minutes later the flight engineer calmly informed me that the oil pressure was dropping on the starboard inner engine as well. This was serious and I eventually lost both engines on the starboard side and had to fly back all the way on the port engines – a tricky business with all the power on one side. I sent an SOS to base to get the flarepath lit in good time but when we arrived over Fayid there was no flarepath and I had to make the circuit and landing in darkness. Luckily in the desert one nearly always had clear starlit nights and I was able to distinguish the main runway and make a landing safely.

Group Captain Turton-Jones remained quite calm throughout the trip although he must have realised that with only two engines running it would be a hazardous landing, if we even got back to base at all. In those days we had no electrically lit flarepaths – they were paraffin lamps which had to be individually lit and it took a long time to get the runway illuminated.

We did a further three trips to Tobruk in August and my total operations numbered thirty-four. (I was rather wondering how much longer Command were going to keep us on operations because in UK the maximum was thirty). However there was to be one more trip and it turned out to be the worst of the Middle Eastern tour.

At that time General Montgomery was building up his armour formations at and behind El Alamein and nearly every week high altitude German photographic reconnaissance planes used to come over from Crete at about 42,000 feet and photograph the whole of the battle zone. There was no means of stopping them because we had no fighter aircraft that was capable of climbing to this height. Churchill had been to the Middle East on a visit and a request was put to him by the Air Force for a Mark X Spitfire and eventually two were sent out to Egypt. These were stripped of all their armour, all but two of the Browning machine guns, and anything else movable that wasn't essential. One took off to attack the Hun reconnaissance aircraft and managed to struggle up to 40,000 feet, but no higher, though the next time it did manage to get within range and shot down the German plane. However, the next day the Hun appeared again and both Spitfires were unserviceable so something drastic had to be done.

Command decided that we should attack the German aerodrome at Heraklion in Crete and endeavour to destroy their reconnaissance planes on the ground in daylight. The operation was planned so that both of our squadrons of Halifaxes would attack at dusk and as there could be no fighter escort because of the distance, we should have the protection of darkness for the return trip. We were briefed on 5th September and bombed up with six 1,000 lb and twelve 250 lb rodded bombs. (These were anti-personnel bombs which had special eighteen inch rods fitted to the nose so that the bomb would explode at ground level.)

Take-off was at 3 p.m. and eighteen loaded Halifaxes took the air, but one aircraft developed engine trouble immediately after take-off and had to hurriedly jettison his bombs in the Bitter Lake. Although the bombs were dropped 'safe' most of them exploded on hitting the water and a British destroyer promptly opened fire at the Halifax with its light guns! The Halifax promptly fired the Very cartridge of the day and there were some rude comments about aircraft recognition! One could hardly blame the Royal Navy, who took great exception to being smothered with eighteen anti-personnel bombs in the middle of a quiet afternoon's snooze!

All seventeen bombers formed up over the aerodrome in vics of three and we set course in tight formation for Crete. Squadron Leader Hank Iveson was leading my vic and I was flying on his port wing and Bickerdike on his starboard wing. Hank was a brilliant pilot and I tucked myself in close, knowing that he would hold a steady course and airspeed. Crete was about 3½ hours from Fayid and we had an uneventful trip across the Mediterranean. Command had made a complete balls-up of the timing and we found ourselves approaching Crete with the sun well up and nowhere near dusk. There was strict wireless silence and one dared not speak for fear of alerting the Hun fighter defences, but Hank signalled to me that he was going to orbit for a while about twenty miles off Crete and all the rest of the formation followed us round. We must have orbited for forty minutes and it seemed an age but eventually we started our bombing run in from south-east to north-west. We could see Heraklion aerodrome clearly and we watched six fighters get airborne which was ominous, but our attention was diverted suddenly with the arrival of heavy flak bursts all round us. Bickerdike and I tucked ourselves in tightly on Hank Iveson and a well-placed shell would have done for the three of us.

Another vic was flying about 70 yards on our port beam and I could see Flight Lieutenant Bryan who was nearest, waving to me, when, suddenly, a heavy shell burst alongside him and his Halifax started to burn. The flames spread along his starboard wing and I could see Bryan giving me the thumbs down signal and waving cheerio; I watched three, four, and then five parachutes billow out of the aircraft and then the starboard wing burned through and fell off the root. The Halifax started a vicious spiral to starboard with black smoke pouring from it and I knew then that Bryan had no chance of baling out. I watched him down to about 8,000 feet when his aircraft started to disintegrate and fall in flaming pieces to the wooded hills below.

Poor Bryan; he and I had been good friends, but death was swift and despite his misfortune my own thoughts were in self-preservation. I looked for a quick moment behind us and saw two more columns of black smoke where another two Halifaxes had been shot down –

the fighters were still not up at our operational height of 16,000 feet; all the damage was being done by heavy and accurate flak.

We then had to concentrate on our bombing run and in keeping tight formation on Hank. Tim Collins was down in the nose waiting for the signal from Hank to bomb. A shell burst just ahead of us and I ducked instinctively as we flew through the black smoke puff, but immediately afterwards our bombs went and Hank began a diving turn to starboard. It was a job to keep our places in formation and Bickerdike fell away to port beneath with the sudden increase in speed.

I was still clinging tight to Hank, and my rear gunner, Jack Croft, was warning me that two Messerschmitt 109's were chasing us from behind. Hank came right down to treetop level over the wooded mountains and we flew very low over the valley. I kept looking behind and there were about five Halifaxes all straggling along behind us, but luckily they were receiving attention from the fighters and not us. Our speed was about 280 mph and we soon found ourselves over the coast and out to sea.

Dusk had just about arrived and it began to be difficult to see the aircraft behind us. One fighter started firing at us from extreme range but he soon broke off the combat and turned back to Crete and safety. Hank gave me the thumbs up sign and indicated that I could break formation; Bickerdike was still some way behind and appeared to be in combat with another fighter but visibility was worsening and we eventually lost sight of him. (Poor old Bickerdike was killed on the first trip of his second tour later.)

As darkness fell I heaved a great sigh of relief, and was glad to have survived the attacks by flak and fighters. We started the long haul back across the Mediterranean. I put the automatic pilot in and asked the radio operator to come and sit in my seat and keep an eye on the instruments while I went down to join Tim. We got out some poker dice and played a game in the half light of his shielded lamp. I suppose it was the result of having escaped with our lives that made us feel so carefree and happy. We got back to Fayid after 7 hours 10 minutes and went into de-briefing.

Of the eighteen aircraft despatched, three had turned back with engine trouble and of the fifteen which attacked Heraklion five had been shot down. The operation had been somewhat costly but considering that Command had slipped on the timing we were lucky not to have suffered heavier losses. Later PRU Mosquitos flew over Heraklion and reported severe damage to hangars and buildings and three of the high-flying German reconnaissance planes had been destroyed on the ground. The operation was an undoubted success because there were no more reconnaissance flights carried out over Egypt.

That completed our thirty-fifth trip and was the last operation of my first tour. I cannot adequately express the utter relief of being rested from operational flying. I was subsequently posted to No 2 Middle East training school as an instructor, still under the command of Wing Commander Young at Aqir. I knew that with luck I should have six months' freedom from operational flying. It was like a last minute reprieve from the death sentence, and life immediately took on a new meaning. I felt exhilarated and happy.

Just at that time we got a telegram from the Air Ministry advising us that Wing Commander Young had been awarded the DSO and I the DFC. Tim and I had been out to dinner at the Greek Club in Ismailia and came back to Aqir full of Chianti and when we walked into the Mess we were greeted with this news. It naturally called for a great celebration, but what mixed with Chianti I didn't know and very foolishly went on to gin and tonics. Jack Croft, my rear gunner, was well away and had quite a good lead on us and so had several of the others who had been in the bar all evening. We all drank far too much to be good for us. Eventually Jack Croft and I started on the journey back to our billet across the sandy stretch outside the Mess. He refused to be supported, declaring that he was quite sober, and the next minute he had disappeared from view! I searched everywhere for him. I knew he couldn't just disappear like that on a smallish stretch of sand so I went back to the Mess and borrowed a torch. I found Jack fast asleep in the bottom of a slit trench. He had apparently fallen down into it when he was walking alongside me and that accounted for his sudden disappearing act!

I was looking forward to sewing on the DFC ribbon. The citation read:

Flight Lieutenant M Renaut is an outstanding Captain of Aircraft. His sorties include attacks on such targets as Frankfurt,

Kiel, Cologne, Brest, Stettin and Essen. He flew with distinction
in both the night raids on the German naval base at Trondheim
on April 27th and 28th last. This officer has constantly been
selected for special operations necessitating a high degree of skill
and reliability; he has never failed to reach the highest expectations. His leadership and courage have been of a high order.
F/Lt. Renaut was born in 1920 in London. He enlisted in 1940
and was commissioned in the following year.

(If only they'd known I damned near failed to reach the highest
expectations!)

We now set about the training of new crews, on the understanding
that none of us would be repatriated until we had trained sufficient
crews to replace the two squadrons. All our pupils were ex-
Wellington pilots so I began the tedious business of circuits and
landings, day in, day out. Our Halifaxes had been modified to
include dual control from the right hand seats, and all through
September and October we were working hard at training new
crews.

Amongst our other jobs was the censoring of other ranks' mail
and this gave me what seemed a bright idea for a practical joke. I
composed a letter purporting to have been written by an AC2
Williams in which I criticised Wing Commander Young and Hank
Iveson, gave away lots of vital information and made a few
suggestive remarks to my wife. I then tucked the letter in amongst
all the other mail one morning. As I expected, it was censored by
one of our officers who promptly took it into Wing Commander
Young's office. I felt it was about time I owned up, but just then I
heard a voice on the aerodrome Tannoy system requesting 'AC2
Williams' to report to the Commanding Officer's office immediately
and at the double! By then the joke had gone too far for me to own
up and I began to wonder what would happen. 'AC2 Williams' of
course never turned up and the joke died a natural death when they
checked up on the names of the station personnel!

Our Arab servants were a dishonest lot and one had to be
constantly alert to their dishonest ways. Because I'd worked at
Lyons I was given the job of Messing Officer. Our diet was very
uninteresting and no one seemed to like the sweet potatoes nor the

unending supply of corned beef, no matter how it was disguised. Corned beef, in fact, formed a large part of our diet and in order to try and make it more appetising I bought a dozen bottles of Worcester sauce and some tomato ketchup. Three days later the Worcester sauce was all finished; and though I began to check up on people during lunch nobody appeared to be helping themselves especially liberally and its disappearance remained a mystery until one day I went into the kitchen and caught an Arab waiter drinking from a Lea and Perrins bottle! The Arabs apparently thought this a very tasty liqueur and no wonder our twelve bottles disappeared so quickly! The bread was frightful and the loaves were full of weevils.

In late October 1942 the great attack at El Alamein began and the request for trained bomber crews increased. I was packing in a lot of flying as the weather was absolutely perfect for it and night flying was a piece of cake with the excellent visibility and starlit nights. I had a very narrow escape one day when I'd flown over to LG 224 with a pupil for circuits and landings. I took off in the left hand seat, and before I was two-thirds of the way down the runway the port inner engine failed. I was ready to make a belly landing in the desert if I could just get airborne and was managing to hold the Halifax at just above stalling speed. But we were heading straight for the pyramids and I couldn't gain even ten feet in height.

I pushed the remaining three throttles wide open through the emergency gate but I had great difficulty in obtaining sufficient power and daren't turn to either port or starboard for fear of stalling. The pyramids drew nearer and I actually flew between them at a little over 100 mph – it was really scorching hot and the Halifax's Merlin engines didn't give of their best in the desert heat. Eventually I flew for about thirty miles in a dead straight line before I was able to climb to about 100 feet and gradually nursed the aircraft round in a slow turn to port. I was very relieved when we landed safely, and so, I think, was my pupil who'd had no hand in the performance.

Christmas was soon upon us and the training school had been moved again to LG 224. Just before Christmas we had the most frightful sandstorm; I had never seen one before and the sight of this brown wall of dust approaching on the skyline was an awesome spectacle. There was a high wind and we started to check on our tent ropes and fasten them down more securely in preparation for what we guessed was to be an unpleasant period. The storm arrived in under the hour and it was absolutely choking – visibility dropped to a few yards and I crawled into my tent to take refuge. At the height of the storm my tent collapsed and nearly smothered me. I was really quite frightened and crawled out of the side choking and half blinded by the dust. I tried to find my way to the mess tent but couldn't see a thing, in the half light. I stumbled upon Wing Commander Young's station wagon, so I hurriedly climbed into the driver's seat and there spent a disturbed night.

I awoke at six with a thick layer of sand upon me. Most of the storm had blown over but there was still a high wind and it was inclined to pick up the loose sand and remain very unpleasant. It was during this sandstorm that the aircraft carrying Lady Tedder (Marshal of the Royal Air Force Lord Tedder's wife) to Cairo crashed when attempting to land at Heliopolis. The aircraft overshot the runway and flew into the side of a hill, exploded and killed everyone on board instantly. Lord Tedder was at the airport to welcome his wife and must have suffered agony in those moments.

The sandstorm blew over before Christmas and on Christmas Day itself all the officers traditionally went to the airmen's mess to serve Christmas dinner. I remember being offered the most gruesome looking drink in an enamel mug. It turned out to be a mixture of beer, sherry, whisky, Cointreau, and creme de menthe, and tasted like nothing on earth – the airman who offered me this brew was quite plastered but he insisted that I drank his health (and my death!). They were happy days and it was a happy station under the command of Wing Commander Young. He was an incredibly good mixer, but never let any junior officer go too far and when necessary was a great disciplinarian.

There was always, though, the acute discomfort of living in a tent; the attempt at washing in a canvas bucket and the sand in one's ears and hair. No wonder we longed for a bath and a bit of hotel luxury. Money was free because there was nothing to spend it on in the desert and I was carefully amassing my bridge and poker winnings for a rainy day. (I was actually in Cairo the day it rained in January 1943 – an almost unheard-of phenomenon.) Tim and I used to hitch-hike into Cairo for a bath and for one shilling one could go to

Wing Commander Renaut, commanding 171 Squadron in 1944.

The improved Halifax after removal of the dorsal turret.

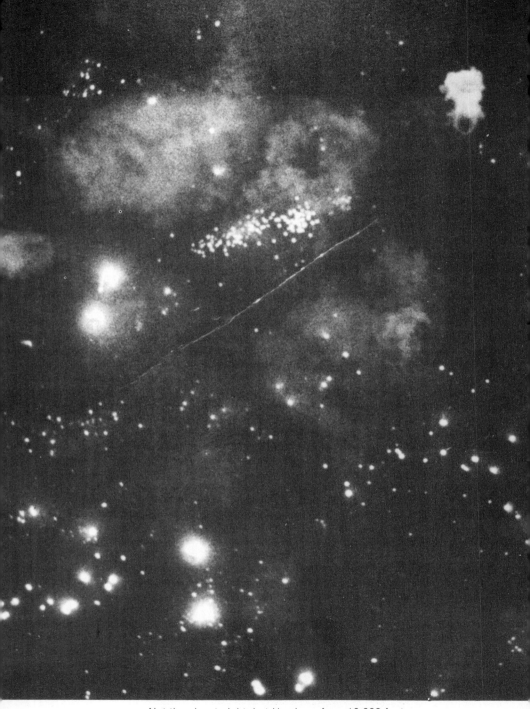

Not the sky at night, but Hamburg from 18,000 feet.

Shepheards Hotel in Cairo and enjoy a bath in a luxurious bathroom with large warm bath towels. We used to eat a colossal dinner afterwards for about 15/- and generally we followed that with a visit across the way to the Bardia night club in Opera Square. This was a clip joint of the first order and one paid heavily for the privilege of watching Egyptian belly dancers. Once we invited one of the girls to our table and she promptly ordered champagne at about £3 a bottle! One night when we were there, there were some very noisy Australians who objected strongly to being clipped and promptly let off a smoke bomb. That cleared the joint in about two minutes flat and we all thought what a good job!

What a city Cairo was! Luxury and squalor, colossal wealth and abject poverty, and always the streams of beggars who literally got under one's feet with their cry of 'Baksheesh'; the native quarter where it was unsafe to venture was out of bounds to all ranks but the more inquisitive used to venture and generally managed to get themselves into trouble with knives or drugs or brawls, and there you would be followed by little Egyptian boys, twelve or thirteen years old, trying to sell their sisters' services with: 'You like my sister? All pink inside like English lady.' There was the usual general supply of flies, and it was quite common to see an Egyptian child asleep in the street with its face literally covered in flies to that the child looked like a negro.

On the brighter side of Cairo there was tea at Groppi's with fabulous cream cakes, dinner at the luxurious Turf Club with its red leather furnishings and superb food; the New Zealand Club where one could take a bath and have one's suit pressed for sixpence, a plate of tomato soup for a penny, and a steak, two eggs and chips for sixpence, buy two ounces of New Zealand tobacco for 2/- and have a packet of cigarette papers given with it. So many things made up Cairo. The dishonest taxi drivers – the first one I met took a pound from me, pretended to reach in his pocket for change and let the clutch in and was gone! The beautiful jewellery shops in the Soliman Pasha, and the fabulous Swiss wrist watches for £6 or £8. The ghastly noisy trams with dozens of Egyptians hanging on by their eyebrows. The silk shops, and my buying rayon and paying the price of silk – I had such a lot to learn! The wonderful officer aircrew club at the top of the tallest building in Cairo run by Leslie

Howard's brother, Arthur Howard. One stayed there in the lap of luxury for £1 per week (it was there that I saw my first Arab conjuror – a man who could make chickens disappear under one's very nose). The foul stench in the back streets and the dirt and squalor of the slums. The eternal begging.

I had learnt a good deal of Arabic from the chief steward at the officers club, including the right phrase for beggars. 'I commit you to Allah' seemed to be the most successful, but other phrases like '*Bokra fil mish mish*' which translated meant 'Tomorrow when the apricots appear' worked wonders in the streets. I remember seeing the film *Mrs Miniver* at the cinema, missing the last lorry back to LG 224 and spending the night in the back of a gharry for 2/6d . . . such discomfort! The nights were warm and muggy and one didn't need a coat on at Christmas. We all enjoyed our Cairo and the mysteries of the East, but always it meant that return to sand and flies at LG 224.

Training and instructing continued and we trained a number of crews in the four months at LG 224. Suddenly one day I felt ill in the air, landed badly and went straight to bed. The MO said I had sandfly fever but it got worse (and so did my flying) until two days later I started passing brown ale instead of urine and became terribly worried. The MO said this time that I had jaundice and I soon began to turn yellow. I was whisked off to a hospital in Cairo and there spent a very pleasant fortnight endeavouring to become bilefree. In the next bed to me was Air Commodore Whitney Straight and a number of other good types in the same room, and life was fun with the nurses. I had a fortnight's leave and recuperated at a club in Alexandria and that, to me, was pure luxury. Alexandria was clean and beautiful and cooler and more open than Cairo – a lovely city in fact, and I spent a most enjoyable fourteen days.

I went back eventually to Fayid, the training unit at LG 224 having disbanded, and Wing Commander Young and the others flown home. I was appointed test pilot at Fayid and was required to test fly aircraft which had crashed and had been rebuilt – a job which I didn't relish very much. Sharing the same aerodrome with us was a cloak and dagger squadron of Liberators. These aircraft were operating at colossal distances over Turkey, Yugoslavia and points north, and were dropping agents in plain clothes. Everything was done in the strictest secrecy and one never saw the agents themselves; they were driven out to the aircraft in closed and curtained cars. I recall once at breakfast in the early morning in the mess seeing a group who had returned because of not receiving the dropping signal in Turkey; they were a motley collection of every nationality including women, but kept themselves to themselves at the breakfast table.

At that time I heard the tragic news that Wing Commander Peter Warner had been shot down in error by one of our own aircraft, a Mosquito, off the Libyan coast. It happened at night and how anyone could have confused a Halifax with a Hun aircraft was beyond me. Poor old Pete, he and I had been such good friends and we had spent many hours together in orange groves. Geoff Thomas, too, had almost killed himself over Greece – he was flying steadily at about 15,000 feet when a flak shell burst under his port wing and blew the Halifax on its back. He lost height with a full bomb load down to 3,500 feet before he regained control. Geoff Raymond was another from the squadron who nearly came to grief – he came back from Benghazi, lost two engines on one side and crash landed at night in the Nile Delta. No one was injured but they were all shaken up.

Then Tim Collins was navigating a Halifax on a night cross-country when they ran out of petrol and force-landed on the sea about half a mile offshore from Jaffa. They were extremely lucky in that the aircraft floated for about forty minutes so they were all able to get out and stand on the wing – the dinghy automatically inflated and they never even got their feet wet! When I saw Tim I asked him if he'd got his Longines RAF watch and he said, 'Yes'.

I told him to tell the authorities that he'd left his watch in the navigator's drawer in the aircraft and to claim another issue. This he did and I got myself a nice watch, but then we heard that they were going to lift the aircraft from the sea bed. I had a sudden panic at the thought that my dishonesty would be detected but luckily the steel hawsers snapped on their attempt to lift the Halifax from the sea bed and the operation had to be abandoned.

I had a great chum who was my wireless operator – an 'Aussie' called Malcolm Street – who was quite a poet in a humorous vein.

He wrote that classic on the Italian Abyssinian campaign which goes like this:

Il Duce give the order to march against the foe,
So off to Ethiopia the organ grinders go,
But now they are unfitted for any sort of grind,
'Cos they're back from Ethiopia with their organs left behind.

The hosts of Ethiopia return to hearth and home,
With knicknacks for the mantelpiece imported straight from Rome.
And the Pope is inundated with pleas to join the choir,
From men whose natural voices are now an octave higher.

Il Duce mounts the rostrum on the regiment's return,
With a noble Roman's ashes in an ancient Roman urn,
For some great gift of gratitude this great occasion calls.
What shall we give our heroes? And the heroes answered 'balls'.

On New Year's Eve I attended a marvellous party as a guest of the Army on board a houseboat on the Nile at Cairo. It was a tremendous affair, and the liquor flowed like water. I regret to report that one of our RAF officers was so sloshed that he fell overboard into the Nile. The cold water sobered him up but he'd shipped so much water by the time he was fished out that he had to have about eight injections from the doctor. The water was filthy and full of diseases. There was a schoolboy howler which said: 'The Mediterranean and the Red Sea are connected by the Sewage Canal.' How very true!

With time now on my hands I was doing a lot of sightseeing before going home and there was a thrill in visiting the ancient biblical sites of Jerusalem, Gaza and the Mount of Olives. It was all very commercialised but nevertheless most impressive and only spoiled by the souvenir sellers and the ever-present beggars. I went to the famous King David Hotel in Jerusalem but could only afford to go in there to pass water, which I did with due reverence. Sad to think that this fine building was later blown up by terrorists.

My test flying at Fayid and LG 224 came to an end in early March and I was posted to No 22 Personnel Transit Camp at Almaza for shipment home.

I can't say I enjoyed the test flying of patched-up wrecks. Every time I took off I feared something would drop off – particularly with Wellingtons and Halifaxes. Sometimes I landed after one quick circuit as the controls weren't responding correctly and handed it back to the fitters to put right. It was an unnerving business and I admire the 'pukka' test pilots of today who face far greater dangers then I ever did.

I was at Farnborough in 1952 when the de Havilland 110 crashed and killed twenty-eight spectators. I had been there on business the first three days and was so impressed with the flying display that I asked my wife Yvonne and the children, a cousin of my wife's and Nigel Bennett and his wife to come along for a picnic in a field on the south side of the aerodrome (I knew that on a Saturday it would be no good trying to get in along with 100,000 other people!) We accordingly parked our cars for half a crown in this farmer's field and sat down to watch the display. Test pilot John Derry and his flight observer had first broken the sound barrier with an enormous supersonic bang and were making a circuit at about 600 mph preparatory to flying low over the crowd when they passed directly over our heads at 200 feet. I was thrilled and stood rooted to the ground whilst Nigel was taking a photograph of the plane. Yvonne, Isabel Bennett, Rosemary and my two children, were rather frightened and, as we watched, the aeroplane suddenly disintegrated directly above us. We were showered with debris and bits of the de Havilland falling all around. Yvonne pushed our two children under the car (they were both crying with fright) and we were all horror-stricken.

The announcer's voice over the loudspeakers simply said: 'Oh my God' and utter silence reigned. We knew John Derry and his observer must have been killed instantly. We hurried to our cars to get away from the scene with all possible speed and eat our picnic disconsolately on Blackbushe Common. It was only later on the six o'clock news that we learned that spectators had been killed and neither Nigel nor I could believe it as we'd seen the tail unit crash 50 yards from us. What we did not know then, of course, was that the front half of the 110 with its two jet engines continued after the main disintegration to hurtle at 600 mph right across the aerodrome. It subsequently crashed near the crowd and the two jet engines ploughed their way onwards into the densely packed crowd on the slopes, killing twenty-eight of them.

I know I was jolly frightened then and so, I believe, was Nigel though we were both hardened to sudden death. Unluckily he had a dud film in his camera and was not able therefore to record the actual first disintegration above our heads. Mr Bishop, one of the chief designers of de Havillands, rang me up on the Monday morning at 8 a.m. to ask me in detail what had happened. I told him I was quite convinced the Perspex nose panel had shattered first. I tried to explain in ten minutes what had actually occurred in one second and I was convinced what I had seen was *fact*. Nigel and I were the only 'airmen' to see the crash so closely but Nigel wasn't sure of what he saw because he had been looking through his camera viewfinder at the moment of disintegration.

I explained to Mr Bishop that after the nose panel had shattered the tremendous force of air ripped open the 110 and caused it to break up. I was absolutely and firmly convinced that what I had seen was fact as I could be reckoned an experienced eyewitness. I never heard from de Havillands again but from discreet enquiries at Farnborough later I learned that part of one wing of the 110 had fallen off earlier (and was found in someone's garden) and this was presumed to have caused the break-up.

I am quite prepared to admit that I was wrong but it shows how even experienced eye-witnesses can be mistaken! To watch something as horrible as that, all occurring within a fraction of a second was very confusing and bewildering. John Derry was a highly skilled pilot and he died doing something he loved, but at the same time paving the way for future development and safety.

How uncanny fear is. I recently flew from London Airport to Leeds and back in an Avro prop-jet. Shortly after leaving Leeds, at 11,000 feet the illuminated sign went on at the bulkhead door leading to the flight deck. 'Fasten your seat belts' immediately followed by a voice saying: 'This is the pilot speaking; will you please fasten your seat belts' (Before he had got any further I was already afraid!) 'as we are about to enter rather turbulent weather conditions'. How silly of me I thought, but no doubt other passengers felt as I did, and I wondered what each person was thinking. It was almost the same thing in war when a rear gunner's voice suddenly broke the silence with: 'Enemy fighter coming in to attack 1,000 yards astern.' My heart *always* sank to my boots but concentration and occupation of one's faculties helped to check this fear.

I often wonder what the reactions would be if on a BEA flight to West Berlin tomorrow a pilot suddenly announced over the loudspeaker: 'This is the captain speaking; we are about to be buzzed by a Russian MIG fighter!' Not that any captain would be silly as to panic his passengers, but it would be interesting to me to watch other people's reactions to such a startling announcement. Of course, airline passengers are not trained bomber crews but they *are* men and women who face some sort of fear every day in their lives. Each and everyone of these imaginary passengers would have reacted differently. Women are just as brave as men in my view – mentally speaking – and they certainly suffer pain more bravely than we, but how would they have reacted? The air hostesses would have probably remained calm; they are trained for the part and are not 'permitted' to show fear!! Some passengers would probably have panicked, some would have had last minute regrets at their shortcomings in life, on the verge of death, some would have remained calm but, I humbly suggest, inwardly terrified. Fear – that 'painful emotion excited by danger' would have made itself felt in a variety of reactions.

I spent days waiting, in common with hundreds of others, for a plane home and used to spend all my days in nearby Cairo. It was at this transit camp that I met an old schoolfriend who had just arrived from England. When he heard I was going home he told me to buy watches, fountain pens and diamonds as they were all in very short supply at home. I took his advice and cashed all my poker winnings and went to my favourite jeweller in Cairo with £145 to buy some watches. I only bought the best makes, Omega, Longines, Movado, Zenith and Rolex and with my money I had no less than seventeen assorted wrist watches. I shied at the thought of buying diamonds because as like as not I would have been swindled, and fountain pens were rather dull so I stuck to watches.

At last news came of a flight home and I was to board a Dakota next day bound for Khartoum – El Pasher – Maidugari – Kano and

Accra. The flight to Khartoum was terribly hot down the length of the Nile; when we landed it was like standing at an open oven door on Regulo '9'! I hardly slept it was so hot but early next morning we boarded the plane for El Pasher and subsequently flew across the heart of Africa to Maidugari. This was an American staging camp and was, of course, excellently run. Unlike El Pasher and Khartoum all the buildings were air conditioned and although we only stopped for an hour while our aircraft was being refuelled, we were each given a packed lunch of cold chicken, salad, new potatoes, ice cream, cheese and biscuits, with a couple of bottles of iced Coca Cola. How typically American! At Khartoum we had eaten the inevitable corned beef and sweet potatoes but this was luxury catering and did we thank our American hosts!

Kano, the next stop, boasted a village market and I went down to inspect the bargains. I bought two lovely twelve foot python snakeskins for a pound and a lovely crocodile handbag for ten shillings. I later heard that before the Americans landed in Africa the snakeskins were only five shillings each! On the flight from Kano to Accra the ground temperature was 130° in the shade and the flight itself was extremely bumpy; I and several others felt terribly sick and we attempted to play bridge to keep our minds occupied. This may seem strange to people who have never flown but the incidence of sickness in the air seems to be related in some way to the extent to which one's mind and body are occupied. I believe that in wartime this theory also applied to the unfortunate aircrew who were castigated as 'Lack of Moral Fibre' cases.

Wireless operators, gunners, bomb-aimers and flight engineers seemed to succumb more frequently than pilots and navigators who, generally speaking, were more fully occupied whilst flying over enemy territory and more particularly over the actual target area. I once had the unnerving experience of my one-time flight engineer literally going berserk in the aircraft just before touch-down. The poor man had to be physically restrained from jumping out of the fuselage door whilst we were travelling at 100 mph along the runway, but even so, as soon as we had slowed down to taxiing speed he hurled himself away from his captors and fled across the aerodrome.

It was unfortunate but the authorities had no option but to be severe and ruthless in cases of 'Lack of Moral Fibre' and though I have no personal experience of the punishment it was rumoured that the luckless man was stripped of his badges of rank in the presence of the entire unit and sent to clean lavatories, for his sins, elsewhere. In a way this was understandable, as cowardice could spread in a squadron if it was not nipped smartly in the bud and if one person got away with it, others would no doubt have followed.

There was one very astute pilot in Bomber Command (who shall be nameless) who gathered his crew together after their first operation over Germany and hatched a plot. He suggested a way for them all to survive their tour of 30 trips and they listened intently as he told them how. Each time they went on an 'op' in future they would take off and climb with the rest of the main force but instead of crossing the coast of Europe they would alter course after dark so that they just flew round in circles over the North Sea, having jettisoned their bombs 'safe'. At the estimated time of arrival back at base they would make sure they joined the circuit long after the first crews had landed, so that when they went to the locker rooms they could hear the crews exchanging stories about the target and learn enough detail to bluff the Intelligence Officer. They could also keep the R/T on 'receive' all the time they were airborne so that they would hear any recall signal or sudden change of target from the 'primary' and 'secondary'. (Other targets were known as 'SEMO and MOPA' (Self Evident Military Objectives and Military Objectives Previously Attacked) – good old Air Ministry stuff!)

Believe it or not this clever ruse fooled the squadron for several 'ops' but eventually the Squadron Commander, together with their flight commander, and the intelligence officer began to have suspicions. They couldn't understand why this aircraft was never damaged by flak and the crew seemed calm and never jittery. To confirm their suspicions and under the strictest secrecy their aircraft had the IFF wired so that when it was switched 'on' it was off and vice versa. (IFF – 'Identification, Friend or Foe' – was a transmitter that recorded on the radar defence screen a different signal from a German plane). You always switched on to IFF some few miles from the coast of Britain on return home to identify you as British. In due course this aircraft was plotted as soon as the wireless operator switched 'off' the IFF and Intelligence followed them round

and round the North Sea for several hours! Whether this was classified
as 'Cowardice in the face of the enemy' or 'Lack of Moral Fibre' or
'Disobeying orders' I never found out, but presumably the Captain
and crew were punished severely. This to my mind was a plot
conceived in fear but implemented with coolness and precision –
they might so easily have completed thirty trips and been awarded
the DFC!

As soon as we landed at Accra I fell in love with the place. It was
right on the sea coast with a lovely off-sea breeze blowing and not
quite on the Equator. We were billeted in the old Police Headquarters and lived a life of luxury whilst waiting for an aircraft to
take us to Takoradi. The fresh fruit was out of this world – melons,
oranges, tropical fruits, bananas ten inches long – and excellent
catering in the mess. There was an outdoor cinema and lovely warm
evenings to sit outside and drink; one had to be careful with
mosquitoes and sleep under a net, which was inclined to be stifling,
but it was not worth risking otherwise. We stayed there for five days
and I was in no hurry to leave. One night I joined a no-limit poker
school of five officers all in transit like me. One hand I was dealt
contained a pair of aces and a pair of fives. The chap on my left
opened the bidding, which was promptly raised by the chap on his
left so I decided to ante and play. I noticed both the others drew two
cards so I felt they were betting on three of a kind. (There were no
wild cards.)

I debated a long while and eventually decided to throw the two
fives and draw three cards in the hope of picking up a third ace. To
my delight I drew the other *two* aces and a Jack and could hardly
believe my eyes or luck. The opener started betting and was
immediately raised by the chap on his left and I was more or less
ignored, having drawn three cards! The betting continued and I was
content to 'see' whilst the other two raised each other but at a later
stage I suddenly raised the betting myself and this caused some
consternation. I continued to raise until eventually I was 'seen' by
the other and collected £35 from the kitty. The chap on my left had
four Queens and I felt terribly sorry for him as in his two cards he
had drawn the fourth Queen; the other chap had a full house – tens
on nines – so I was somewhat unpopular at having got the kitty after
drawing three cards. In a straight game of poker I have never seen

three hands of such worth. Being a transit camp the kitty was composed of a variety of currency and I picked up Egyptian pounds, American dollars and English coin all jumbled together on a rough and ready exchange basis.

After five days we were transported by Dakota to Takoradi, the American staging post for the Middle East, and there we boarded a small and smelly cargo boat for Freetown. It was a five day trip in convoy with an escort of a destroyer and one Sunderland flying boat. We had an uneventful trip except for a suspected Italian submarine on our third day out; the Sunderland dropped four depth charges but we neither saw nor heard any definite result. The food on board was appalling and I got absolutely sick of the eternal corned beef for breakfast, lunch and dinner, the sweet potatoes and tea made with evaporated milk. Thank God the ship had liquor so we drowned our sorrows and did little else but play bridge and poker in the wardroom.

As we arrived in Freetown harbour we could see the vast *Mauretania* anchored off-shore and this was to be our transport home. We got wind that she was a dry ship so we equipped ourselves with whisky and gin at about 8/- per bottle and knew that any tonics or soda water would be available on board the *Mauretania*. We went on board and were shown our berths. I, as a flight lieutenant, was in a single cabin modified to sleep nine and the atmosphere in the strict blackout could be cut with a knife. I used to sleep with my watches under my pillow in case we were torpedoed. The *Mauretania* was quite a fast ship and, of course, sailed alone and not in convoy . . . she made about 28 knots in the open sea and we were scheduled to take seven days to Liverpool. The food was quite superb but there were always two sittings at meals because there were 7,000 on board and the ship was built to take 1,200! We spent the RAF's twenty-fifth anniversary on board and they laid on a special dinner in our honour. The ship's passengers were mainly army from India but there was a big male and female contingent as well as a number of survivors from the *Empress of Britain* which had been torpedoed not far off Freetown.

The OC troops on board was an army colonel and he was a magnificent organiser; we had dancing every evening, ship's concerts, bridge drives, Housey Housey or 'Bingo' and talent spotting etc., and the time passed very quickly. After we had been at sea for three days I got Tim Collins to take a sextant reading of our course and after much deliberation he informed us that we were heading due south! We called him a rotten navigator but he insisted that we were heading fast in the wrong direction. (We later heard that the *Mauretania* actually sailed south and south-west for a whole day to avoid a gaggle of U-boats in her path off Spain – so Tim had been right.)

We used to play bridge most of the day, Tim and I, but it was always a job to get a free table in the 1st class lounge. We soon learned the dodge of rushing to the port beam and shouting: 'Land, land!' There was a general stampede to have a look-see and if you were quick you got a table! We later ran very late and after eight days there was still no sign of land, we got into a frightful North Atlantic gale in mid-March which was most unpleasant.

All the RAF officers on board were required to do spells of duty on the bridge as aircraft spotters and I found it jolly cold in the early morning. The sea was hellish rough and with a sixty knot gale in our face it literally became impossible to work round to the bows of the ship. I felt very sorry for the other ranks who were jammed head to toe in the bowels of the ship and people were being sick everywhere to make matters worse.

On the ninth day, still in rough weather, we saw land on the port side! This was most unexpected but there was no doubt that what we could see was the Mull of Galloway and it appeared that we had sailed right round the north coast of Ireland and were heading down towards Liverpool. The *Mauretania* made for shelter in the Isle of Man for the ninth night and on the tenth day we sailed up the Mersey into Liverpool – our first sight of Britain since July 1942. I began to have qualms about my seventeen watches and at the last moment I was so worried about the forthcoming customs examination that I sold three of the watches on board for a very good profit. We disembarked and were led into the huge customs shed where a customs officers announced over the loudspeaker that there would be no customs examination because Liverpool was being bombed and they were anxious to get us away to the transit camps as quickly as possible. I was most relieved at this news and felt up my ankles and wrists to make sure all my watches were still there! Tim and I eventually caught a train to London where we enjoyed fourteen days leave. I went to several London jewellers and sold my fourteen watches at between 250 and 300% profit. I then wished, of course, that I had bought more but later considered that I had been fortunate.

Looking back over the long trip home the most enjoyable part had been our stay at Accra and I've often had a hankering to go back. I had a marvellous African servant in my room at Accra who had a great beaming smile and a great sense of humour. He was called Sambo, which wasn't surprising, but his efforts at giving service were wonderful and every morning he brought my clothes to me all laundered and ironed from the night before. On my last morning in Accra I asked him what tip officers usually left and he said: 'Bad masters give me two shillings Sah; good masters give me one pound.' I accordingly left him ten shillings (striking, as I thought, the happy medium!) but to check on his honesty I asked the President of the Mess Committee at breakfast whether the African was speaking the truth. He replied: 'Good God, no! – give him two cigarettes and he'll be overjoyed. Don't for heaven's sake give him a pound or he'll retire and never work again!' I didn't inform him that my servant would probably go into 'semi-retirement' as a result of my generosity!

On the ship that took us from Takoradi to Freetown there had been a very charming Indian doctor called Mehta and he had a beautifully hand-made wooden tray incorporating a hundred different types of wood. He asked me if I would take the tray home with me and deliver it to his wife in Bayswater. I took great care of the tray and kept it behind the pillow in my bunk on the *Mauretania* but after we'd left the customs shed I suddenly remembered it. I asked the coach to wait and ran all the way back to the docks and boarded the *Mauretania*, went to my cabin and retrieved the tray! It was only afterwards that I realised I'd done all this without being stopped or checked; it would have been easy for me to have planted a bomb on the *Mauretania* for all anybody cared.

In due course I handed over the tray to Mrs Mehta who was thrilled with it. (Three years later, when I was living in London, my wife had an internal haemorrhage at one o'clock in the morning and I badly needed a doctor but didn't know one in London. I suddenly remembered Dr Mehta, and quickly looked him up in the telephone directory and found his number. He remembered me and very kindly turned out and rushed to our house in Bayswater Road. He made a quick and correct diagnosis and called in a famous gynaecologist from Harley Street all in the space of half an hour. An ambulance was called (the only time I've ever dialled 999) and an emergency operation performed in Putney Hospital. I shall always remember Dr Mehta for what he did and be eternally grateful.)

CHAPTER V

Halifax Conversion Unit

After my leave I was posted to Marston Moor, near York, as a flying instructor on Halifaxes on a heavy bomber conversion course. Group Captain Cheshire was the Station Commander and I was pleased to see him again – we had a long chat in his office and he told me that David Young was the Station Commander of nearby Rufforth and that he'd made a request to have me there. I therefore only spent a day at Marston Moor and next day reported to Rufforth and Group Captain Young. Our job was to train crews for No 4 Group (Bomber) in Yorkshire and I was appointed as a deputy flight commander in the rank of flight lieutenant under Squadron Leader Iveson.

Rufforth was a temporary station with a Nissen hut mess but we were billeted in Rufforth Hall, a lovely house about two miles from the aerodrome and about 4½ miles from York. Our chief flying instructor was an Australian named Wing Commander Bob Norman and he and I were to get along very well together. Early in May I was promoted to squadron leader, and at last I was entitled to transport of my own. We used Matchless motor-cycles for our journeys between the aerodrome and Rufforth Hall and I never really got to like them. Hank Iveson was a crack rider and sometimes I used to ride as his pillion passenger, I was scared to death at the vicious way he cornered . . . one might almost have thought that Hank was doing fighter affiliation on his motorbike!

We were a very happy unit at Rufforth but the population amongst the instructors was always changing as after roughly six to nine months instructing they were posted back to squadrons for their second tour of operations. The intake of pupils was constant and one met a number of very interesting types – Canadians, Australians, New Zealanders, Americans, French, Poles and Norwegians all passed through our hands. The course embraced circuits and bumps, three engined flying, fighter affiliation, formation flying, bombing practice, steep turns and cross-country flights and so long as the weather remained fine enough to fly, we flew.

The strain of instructing was considerable but, of course, it didn't compare with the strain of operational flying. Our aircraft consisted entirely of planes thrown out by the operational squadrons after they'd done 1,000 flying hours, and at times they were very unreliable. Our engineering officer, Squadron Leader Rolfe, was a first class man and thanks to his excellent organisation we nevertheless enjoyed at Rufforth a high percentage serviceability among our Halifaxes. The fact remained, however, that they were mostly clapped out old junk and some of them wouldn't hold altitude on two engines on one side. Some others didn't seem powerful enough on take-off and one night I was giving instruction on 'circuits and bumps' to a nervous pupil who obtained full power too late and I had grave doubts as to whether we'd become airborne. It was pitch dark and I knew there was a thick wood 300 yards from the end of the runway which ruled out a wheels-up 'belly-flop'. Unfortunately we were past the 'point of no return' on the runway and there was nothing for it but to press on and pray.

Unfortunately my pupil was terrified we weren't going to make it and in his fear he 'froze' on to the controls. In other words he had hold of the control column like Samson and no amount of wresting with the dual controls on my part had any effect. He was only small but immensely strong (all this was happening within five seconds) and we were doing 90 mph at the last 100 yards of runway. A split second decision had to be made, and though I hated doing it I hit him hard in the face and he promptly let go.

I grabbed the dual control column and lugged the Halifax off the ground and banged the throttles through the emergency boost gate and we just made it, skimming the tops off the trees! Funnily enough he was all right the next take-off but I warned him I'd hit him harder if he 'froze' again. I explained that in fact I was just as frightened as he and I think it helped him. Anyway he had to repeat the process immediately else he might never have made the grade. (I wonder what happened to him when he joined an operational squadron.)

There were the inevitable crashes which at times were sickening

Cologne 1945.

Cologne 1945.

but this was to be expected with crews fresh from the operational training units. I remember one night a pupil crew doing circuits and landings, and on their first landing the aircraft developed a swing to port. The pilot over-corrected with use of the port outer engine and swung off the runway hitting the 'Chance light' (used to illuminate the runway). The starboard engine hit the chance light and burst into flames and evidently they all panicked and made for the fuselage door, leaving the port out throttle wide open. The result was that the aircraft started to orbit on its axis and by now the whole of the starboard wing was ablaze – petrol streamed out of the burning tanks and made a ring of burning fuel on the ground so that none of the crew could jump clear. This weird performance continued for fully three minutes. Eventually the starboard undercarriage collapsed and still the aircraft orbited to starboard. It was now a mass of flames and the crew had to abandon the aircraft and make a run for it. But the back of the aircraft broke, the fuselage by the main spar was burning fiercely and the poor navigator didn't make it. He got left behind and was soon overcome by the flames and burned to death. It was a disgraceful accident, the blame for which rested squarely on the pilot's shoulders as he had left one of the throttles wide open when he hurriedly left the controls. On the other hand he was inexperienced and fire in an aircraft is a horrible thing to witness.

Later that month I was appointed President of a Court of Enquiry into a bad accident to one of the Halifaxes from Marston Moor (then under the command of Group Captain G.L. Cheshire vc, dso, dfc). The aircraft had dived into a golf course from 1,500 feet for no known reason during night flying. I made all the usual enquiries of what few eye-witnesses there were and they all contradicted themselves with their evidence. Some said an engine was on fire before the crash, others said it started to break up in the air, but they were most civilians who didn't know the front of an aeroplane from the back and their evidence was worse than useless.

I was given the assistance of a young engineer officer and four groundcrew with spades and we started to dig our way down into the large crater the aircraft had made. The greater part of the Halifax was eighteen feet deep and the stench of charred human flesh was nauseating – the poor engineer officer was violently sick when we came to the bodies. They were all seven packed tight into the nose of the aircraft, headless and limbless and the stench was awful. We had to be very careful with cutters and implements because there was a great deal of unburnt petrol about and we didn't want another fire. Spectators from the village started to gather round and I had to call on the police to have them dispersed. How mothers could bring their small children to look at the carnage was beyond me and I felt pretty nauseated myself.

We couldn't lift the bodies by hand so we had to get a crane to tug them clear and the sight of these trunks being hoisted clear by a crane was sickening. It took us a whole day to get the seven dead men out and, that completed, we continued digging to get at the four engines so that we might get a clue as to what had happened. Still the villagers kept morbidly looking-on, fascinated, and again I had to ask the village constable to keep them back. They were watching our every move. Even when I found two unburnt fingers by the top of the crater they kept watching the crane pulling out the charred trunks with fascination.

We eventually dug down (by hand) to the bottom of the crater and found the first Merlin engine 22 feet deep. The Halifax, I presumed, had dived vertically into the soft ground from 1,500 feet and I felt the only explanation was a faulty elevator control, though I could not substantiate this on evidence, and the findings of a Court of Enquiry had to be backed up by real evidence and facts, not conjecture. I remember putting in my report: 'We were unable to establish the cause of the accident on factual evidence but it is the opinon of the President that a likely cause was failure of the elevator control.' (I was even criticised for putting this in my report!) Like so many Courts of Enquiry where there were no survivors we came to a dead end and were unable to establish the cause of the crash.

We had another bad one near Rufforth Hall the next week. I heard the Halifax crash when I was dressing at Rufforth Hall and quickly jumped on my motorbike and rode to the spot. The fire tenders had not yet arrived and the aircraft was burning fiercely on the ground. (I was the first there.) Some of the crew were still inside but the heat of the fire prevented me from going to their aid. Suddenly one member of the crew extricated himself and jumped to the ground from the top escape hatch. Just as he landed a petrol tank burst over him and he was incinerated where he lay. It was weird because he landed on all fours and was petrified in that position and burned down to the size of a monkey.

The ambulance crew and fire tenders eventually arrived from the aerodrome but there was nothing they could do except wait for the fire to abate. The bodies were wrapped in blankets and again no one could say the cause of the crash – the only witnesses were all burned to death and would never speak again. I began to have a loathing of fire and dreaded my own aircraft ever exploding into flames – the sight of the black pall of smoke and the noise of exploding ammunition and oxygen bottles were altogether too familiar. They all had a certain smell about them too which defied description.

In June 1943 we held a mess party and dance at Rufforth and one of the flight commanders, Chick Whyte, told me that he'd invited a couple of nurses from the Nursing Home in York. He asked me if I'd like to partner one called Yvonne Campbell and I readily agreed. When she arrived, a smallish attractive brunette with a lovely figure, I was introduced and immediately fell for her! I naturally believed in love at first sight for I was terribly smitten and danced every dance with her. Before the dance was over I knew that I wanted her to be my wife. Understandably the same thoughts were not running though her mind and I had rather an uphill struggle.

After the dance I saw her back to the Purey Cust Nursing Home in York and didn't dare risk kissing her goodnight. I felt a bit of a lemon shaking hands but then I didn't want to rush things at first! I asked her if I could see her again and got a 'Yes'. We made a date for the next night and I could hardly sleep with excitement. There was absolutely no doubt in my mind by then that I wanted to marry her, but unfortunately she had other boyfriends and it wasn't going to be easy.

The next evening couldn't come quickly enough and I met her outside the Nursing Home as arranged. We went to the well known De Grey rooms in York to dance and had a long chat about each other. She told me that she'd always lived in Brussels until the Huns marched in Belgium and that she was engaged to a Belgian boy who was in the Army. I didn't reckon much on my chances as she seemed very much in love with this Zizi Gregoire and they wrote to each other frequently through diplomatic channels. We went and sat by the river in York and talked for hours, but still I didn't dare to kiss her or even put my arm around her which I was longing to do! She must have thought me a slow worker but I'd had no experience worth talking about and this was definitely the girl for me, but how to go about it? She was due then to go on a spell of night duty and that put an end, temporarily, to our meetings.

We continued with the usual routine of flying instruction and fresh crews kept the interest alive. One afternoon Geoff Thomas was overdue from a flight of two-engined flying instruction with a pupil and I began to be worried. Later the Royal Observer Corps reported a Halifax crashed in the Yorkshire Wolds but there were no survivors. This turned out to be Geoff Thomas's aircraft and the shock nearly did for me – to be killed instructing was a frightful thought, but it did happen apparently. I was called upon to verify that a blackened wrist watch belonged to Geoff Thomas – but this was all the Court of Enquiry were able to find. The funeral was a most depressing affair; I still couldn't get really used to the death of close friends – Geoff's death quite shattered me.

Hank Iveson had a narrow escape in August; he was giving instruction, was throwing the Halifax all over the sky and when he landed the aircraft was taken over by another crew on the same exercise. The new crew had only been airborne for a few minutes when the starboard wing came clean off at 2,000 feet. The accidents investigation branch came down to examine the wreckage in which eight men had been killed instantly and they found that a main wing bolt had sheared in flight, causing the wing to break off at the root. Poor Hank Iveson went white as a sheet when he heard the news, for he had been in the same aircraft a few minutes earlier! Such was life.

We had a very competent senior administration officer at Rufforth by the name of Squadron Leader Wilson, who was a go-getter and a man for getting things done. After six months in Yorkshire I was able to mimic the accent and one day rang him up pretending to be a Yorkshire builder. I told him that it had come to my knowledge that he had been purloining bricks stacked on a building site just outside the aerodrome and what was he going to do about it! Wilson was very frightened and most apologetic and claimed that he had thought the bricks were RAF property. I told him this was nonsense and that he would be hearing from my solicitors. Poor man, he was genuinely worried and looked quite upset when I saw him in the Mess!

I found out that Squadron Leader Wilson was so frightened at 'borrowing' the bricks that he went to Group Captain Young and asked his advice. Apparently he was having built a small office without calling upon RAF funds and as there were thousands of bricks nearby he felt that the contractors wouldn't miss a few hundred. The laugh was on me when I eventually got married – and Wilson turned up at our wedding dressed as an Arab and carrying a hod of bricks! When I saw this character approaching at the reception I didn't even recognise him and thought madly about whom I knew in Egypt who had turned up at my wedding!

Another hoax I pulled was on Flight Lieutenant Fred Ammon (now working at London Airport control centre) who was our Flying Control Officer under Squadron Leader Timothy Tame at Rufforth. I rang him up one evening in the Control Tower when all was quiet and impersonated the Yorkshire accent. I said to Ammon: 'I've got 10 tons of coke for you (Flying Control was heated by coke boiler) – where do you want it put?' Ammon replied that he couldn't possibly accommodate 10 tons of coke anywhere! I said that he'd have no coke for the whole winter unless he took in the delivery and poor old Fred reluctantly agreed. The following day, in the mess, he said to Wilson his coke had not turned up but when it did what would Group Captain Young think of the mess outside his control tower? As far as I know, Fred Ammon still doesn't know what became of his 10 ton delivery.

Yvonne came off night duty and I began again to press my suit. She asked me home to meet her parents in Market Weighton, a small market town twenty miles from York on the Hull Road, and I felt that this was some improvement. I was terribly in love with her and any headway I managed to make was encouraging. Her parents kindly went out and left us alone and I'm proud to say that I managed a kiss or two whilst we sat on the sofa. In fact we became engaged in November and celebrated with two cups of cocoa . . . drink being so scarce.

It was in Market Weighton that I first met Ernest Sugden who taught me the art of pigeon shooting. He was a champion shot and had got the business of killing wood pigeons down to a fine art. He earned his living as a sugar beet valuer and naturally this meant calling at farms in the East Riding. His many contacts led to many desperate phone calls asking him to come and deal with the pigeons. Some farmer would ring up to complain that his field of peas was smothered in wood pigeons and Ernest and I would set out early in the morning complete with wire netting, spruce, spades and spikes and dig ourselves a hide near a hedgerow. We would then set out a dozen decoys, drive the car some distance away under the trees and settle down in our hide to wait.

The first birds would fly in soon afterwards and from a very restricted opening in the hide we would fire our first shots. Any birds killed Ernest would peg out in amongst the decoys until we had maybe two dozen birds down in front of the hide. On our best day, shooting for something like ten hours, we bagged 165 wood pigeons and these fetched 4s 9d each in the London markets. When we'd tired of it we used to bag the pigeons up and send them by train to London and back would come the cheque by return. With meat rationing so severe the pigeons fetched good prices. Even rooks, magpies, crows and plovers which got in the way were similarly treated and would themselves fetch 1s or 1s 3d. We later heard our pigeons would turn up on the London restaurant tables as 'Irish Grouse' – an elevated status for the humble wood pigeon.

Ernest was very kind to me during the years I knew him in Yorkshire and being one of the lucky ones with an unlimited supply of petrol for his job, he used to run me back to Rufforth in the early morning so that I could spend the night at Yvonne's home. He later left this country with his wife and family and settled in Rhodesia where he farmed and grew tobacco. He was a beautiful shot and with a twelve bore, he, Trevor Field (England Champion shot at one time) and I used to have many wonderful days out on the Yorkshire Wolds. I recall one occasion in January when they invited me wild goose shooting on the River Humber near Selby by moonlight. We took up our positions in a dyke and set out the decoys in a stubble field in front of us. We then stood and waited for the birds to come in and feed. It was perishingly cold and the dyke we were standing in was ice covered. I completely lost the feeling of both my feet in the waiting period and Ernest and I smoked to try and keep warm. Trevor was in another dyke some 200 yards away and at about 1.30

in the morning we heard the first geese coming off the river to feed.

What a thrill it was to see the flights of geese in the air; Ernest, who was an expert, called the geese in and the first vic formation wheeled towards us and came in to land amongst the decoys. They were perfectly silhouetted against the moonlight and the first two birds were easy meat. However, after firing once, the geese scattered wildly in the night air and the second barrel was a vastly different proposition. We went on shooting for as long as the geese came into feed and when we packed up we'd shot no less than thirty-eight of them. They made lovely eating but the majority of them we sent to London for the money.

Christmas was upon us at Rufforth and the training slackened for the general festivities of the holiday. Christmas Eve was a bit hectic in the Mess and several people drank far too much to be good for them, amongst them Flight Lieutenant Sam Hartley. He was offering people a pull from a full whisky bottle but no one obliged; so in a fit of showmanship he tipped the bottle back and drank the complete contents in two draughts! I thought he'd collapse, but not a bit of it – he asked me if he could borrow my motor-cycle and promptly rode back to Rufforth Hall to sleep it off. I was so concerned that I went back about eight o'clock to see how he was and there was Sam collapsed on the stairs outside his room! He was out to the world so I heaved him on to his bed and let him sleep it off whilst I went back to the Mess. I was a fool to have let Sam use my motor-bike after drinking practically a whole bottle of Scotch but he seemed so stone cold sober and, after all, it was only 1½ miles to the Hall. Looking back Sam could have collapsed on the bike and killed himself or someone else but I never thought of the risk I was running. Sam Hartley was killed on his second tour of ops.

We had another type in the Mess, a pupil named Squadron Leader Richardson who had the greatest capacity for whisky I have ever known. He used to stand at the bar when it opened at mid-day and drink whisky till 2 p.m. I used to say to him: 'Tony, what about your lunch?' And back came the usual reply: 'I never eat on an empty stomach, old boy.' He was a character, but seldom got drunk despite his phenomenal intake of alcohol.

Another charming man was Wing Commander Iles who was in charge of the Silloth Trainer. (He'd designed it himself – a sort of

aeroplane fuselage and cockpit with controls operated by air
bellows for instruction on instrument flying). The 'Link Trainer'
was the standard RAF mock up of an aircraft with a set of normal
instruments and controls and would record a pupil's flight on
graph paper so that his faults could be analysed afterwards. You sat
inside this little 'box', hot and stuffy, and it was the nearest thing to
night flying that could be reproduced. The 'Silloth Trainer' was
Gordon Iles' brainchild and it consisted of a Halifax fuselage,
controls etc., but no wings. The whole contraption was worked by
organ bellows and simulated actual flight much more accurately
and realistically than the Link Trainer (hence Gordon's ability to
play the organ). Crews were actually able to carry out cross-country
flights in the Silloth, the navigator plotting courses and changes of
wind etc.,

Wing Commander Iles must have had a brilliant brain. He lives
somewhere in Earls Court, I believe, and is still probably playing
the organ beautifully. He was one of the most popular members of
the Mess and had a wonderful sense of humour. I remember once
four of us going into York Minster and Gordon Iles, who was really a
brilliant organist, asked if he might play the organ. The Minster
official looked at us four RAF officer aircrew and the thought must
have gone through his mind that we were going to 'swing it' but in
the end he reluctantly let Gordon play. After only a few bars he was
convinced, and we stayed an hour listening to an organ as it should
be played.

Iles was later posted to a unit in the south and we were all heart-
broken to lose him. David Young and I jokingly said that we were
going to tie a label round his neck marked 'Return to Rufforth' in
case he should come to grief in his car! He must have been psychic,
for Gordon Iles had a bad car smash in the outskirts of Tadcaster.
He was apparently driving quite fast into the sun and completely
failed to see a red traffic light and collided with another car coming
across. He was admitted to York Hospital in due course, and later,
when he'd recovered he returned to Rufforth for good and all, the
previous posting having been rescinded. We were all delighted to
have him back and the occasion naturally called for great celebration.
Dear old Gordon . . . I wonder where he is now?

In January we had another spectacular crash at Rufforth. I was officer in charge of night flying and the senior flying control officer was handling the circuits and bumps. We had a request for permission to land from a Halifax which was duly given and another Halifax was taxiing to the take-off point ready for take off. The control officer held him there whilst the first Halifax cleared the runway and after perhaps two minutes the take-off aircraft was given the clear to go. He was halfway down the runway under full power when the pilot of the first Halifax suddenly announced he was stuck on the runway with a burst tyre! Panic! – we fired a red Very cartridge in an effort to stop the Halifax from taking off but it was too late and we heard this frightful bang two-thirds of the way down the runway and a Halifax careered up in the air crazily but managed to fly on. We climbed in a car and drove madly down the runway to the scene of the accident, sloshing our way through gallons of petrol.

When we got there we found a terrified crew running in all directions! They had heard this aircraft taking off and realised too late that they were in the way and madly disembarked and fled. The Halifax taking off just became airborne and was in the act of retracting the undercarriage when it hit the Halifax on the ground. Its undercarriage cut through the port wing and ripped it off, spraying petrol everywhere and a large chunk of the tail plane hit the running flight engineer in the back of the neck and floored him. That was the only casualty, whereas there might have been the most frightful carnage had the Halifax taking off not become airborne. The aircraft made two circuits of the aerodrome and received permission over the R/T to belly land on the cross wind runway. This he did amid a shower of sparks but the landing was made at too high a speed and the Halifax overshot the end of the runway and went straight over a gun pit. The gun pit was manned by the RAF Regiment who were all fast asleep, luckily, and the incredible thing is that the three of them all slept through the crash and knew nothing about it until they were shown the remains of the Halifax fifty yards beyond them!

In February I had my first real crash, whilst giving three-engined landing instructions at Pocklington aerodrome, near York, I had a pupil named Sergeant Sproat who was quite able but terribly nervous and lacked confidence, and he was carrying out a three-engined landing and made a complete mess of the approach. I told him to overshoot and go round again but he was slow opening the throttles and our airspeed dropped to around 90 mph in a gradual turn to starboard against the dead engine. After only seconds our speed dropped to 80 mph with full flap and undercarriage partly retracted, and by the time I was able to take over from the right seat we were bound to force-land. I looked everywhere for a suitable field but as luck would have it there was nothing except a ploughed field with a big chestnut tree on the approach – it had to to be this and I plunged through the top of the tree smashing the Perspex all round me, stuck the nose down hard, held off and held my breath, and sat the old Halifax down in the middle of the ploughed field.

I was thrown forward on impact as I wasn't strapped in, the mud was flying everywhere, two engines tore off at their mounting and we miraculously came to rest without injury to anyone on board. I was really terrified of fire and told the crew of seven to abandon as quickly as possible and I was the last out, in a hurry! Thank God, although the Halifax was smouldering, we didn't burn or explode.

It was a somewhat unnerving experience and I felt quite shaken about. Crash tenders and an ambulance arrived from Pocklington aerodrome and we were given a lift back to base and I was feeling rather guilty at being responsible for the loss of a £70,000 aeroplane. Group Captain Young was very nice about it and put it down to unfortunate circumstances – we were lucky not to have stalled and dived in; that could have been the end of all of us like Geoff Thomas and his crew.

I felt considerably unnerved and shocked the next day and quickly did a few circuits and bumps in a Halifax to restore my confidence, but it was some days before I stopped thinking of how nearly we'd all died. If the Halifax had stalled at 90 mph we would have been killed instantly or burned to death slowly. (The report given by David Young to Group H.Q simply summed up by saying 'Pilot Error' and I felt a bit narked that I had to carry the can as captain of the aircraft but undoubtedly a contributory factor was the fact that this ex-operational clapped out Halifax was slightly underpowered.) Coupled with this I was sitting in the right hand seat and this made flying somewhat unnatural and akin to driving a left-hand drive car in London. We hit the ground mighty hard that day but if it had not been for this 65 foot chestnut tree I could have put her down more gently. Luckily the top branches were thin and brittle – as it was they smashed the Perspex and glass screen. (After that I always used safety straps as I nearly knocked myself out when we hit the ground at 85 mph and I might easily have been thrown out and killed.)

February was a lucky month for weather and we flew practically every day. I had one very interesting pupil, an American named Lieutenant Kornegay – he was a cattle rancher in Texas and could roll a cigarette one-handed. He gave me a packet of his American tobacco and it was like chopped herbs in a little linen bag! How on earth he managed to roll them one-handed (and on horseback he claimed!) was a mystery to me. I was very jealous of Kornegay.

Our wedding, planned for 11th March, drew nearer and I began to get childishly excited. My fears were practically non-existent – I was now an instructor, I was getting married, I loved Rufforth and the life, there was no prospect of going back on my second tour of operations – I was really happy and had not a serious care in the world. We were married at 2 p.m. at the church of St Michael le Belfry, next to York Minster, and it was a wonderful (but windy!) day. The reception was held at the home of our Air Officer Commanding, Air Vice-Marshal Roddy Carr (he was related to Yvonne by marriage) and I, the husband, think I enjoyed myself more than anyone else! My parents and Yvonne's parents were both there, fifty RAF officers, and who should turn up, (as I said) dressed as an Arab and carrying a hod of bricks, but Squadron Leader Wilson whose leg I'd pulled about thieving bricks!

Richard Oakes was my best man, and turned up on crutches, saying that he'd fallen off the wing of a Sunderland. (It seemed an unlikely story and I later discovered that he and two others had been the only survivors of twenty men in a Sunderland that crashed in Scotland in similar circumstances to the Duke of Kent.) I made the first speech of my life, which consisted almost entirely of thanking people for their presents and for the wonderful day. Later I was carried out shoulder high by Bill Kofoed, Sam Hartley, Flight Lieutenant Wilson, Group Captain Young and a whole crowd of other Rufforth people to the waiting hired car which was to take us to York Station. We had planned our honeymoon in Edinburgh and

Largs and it was impossible to keep our departure point a secret. York Station became like a funfair with confetti, rude words chalked on the sides of the carriage, people shouting and climbing on and off the train and complete bedlam until the train finally pulled out!

I was so happy and so in love that I didn't care who knew it, but poor Yvonne was desperately trying to look as though she'd been married for years whereas whenever I stood up to put a case on the rack, confetti poured out of me! The people in the compartment smiled benignly and we went happily on our way. We arrived at Edinburgh at 9.45 p.m. and made straight for the North British Hotel where, thanks to the late Lord Nuffield, operational aircrew were housed at £1 a day all in. After four days there we moved on to the Marine Hotel at Largs and were made very welcome. Yvonne was still most anxious for us to look like a steady married couple and I kept putting up blacks like asking her whether she took sugar in her tea! Being newly married was a thrill to me and I didn't care who knew it.

After fourteen glorious days we returned to Yorkshire, Yvonne again to her night duty at the Nursing Home and me to my instructing at Rufforth. It was a strange beginning to our married life: I used to kiss Yvonne goodnight as she went on night duty and I went back to my quarters at Rufforth Hall – 1½ miles away! In those days I had no car, only a motorbike on which civilians weren't allowed, so I went everywhere by taxi. York taxis would only go a maximum of three miles radius because of petrol rationing so it meant 'asking nicely' to be taken to Rufforth at 1/- per mile, or 9/- fare. One night after saying good night to Yvonne I got, after persuasion, a taxi to the Hall and the driver charged me 30/-. I said: 'How much?' rather taken aback and he said, 'Well, I'm outside the limit and we can charge what we think.' So I got out an old envelope from my pocket, wrote on it, 'I certify that I drove S/Ldr. Renaut from York to Rufforth (4½ miles) and charged him 30/- fare. Signed . . . . . ' The taxi driver refused to sign and I refused to pay 30/- so in the end he went off with 9/- talking about ingratitude of aircrew. The same firm overcharged me £4 for taxis at our wedding so I took the bill to a friend of mine, the chief of police at York, and he got me my money back. What 'clippers' those taxi-drivers were!

After a long search we managed to rent a small house at Acomb near York and Yvonne was installed and managed terribly well. It was only 3½ miles from Rufforth and I used to live out and go to and fro on my motorbike very happily.

There was still no news of my going back on my second tour of operations and I heard very second-hand that Air Vice-Marshal Carr had been kindly persuaded to allow me to remain at Rufforth a bit longer so that we could enjoy a little married life before facing death once again.

On 20th April 1944 I was sent on a Commanders' Course to Cranwell and I realised that being selected for this meant that something was in the wind. It was only a three weeks course but terribly well run and was a great experience. We all wore our names on our lapels and quite obviously were being watched closely and it tended to make one rather self-conscious. There were fifty of us on the course and we were worked very hard – drill, lectures, debates, classes etc., and our only relaxation was a trip to the dull town of Sleaford which boasted no less than forty-three pubs! I remember one debate when the motion was: 'That this house considers that the pilot is the only fit person to captain an aircraft.' After a good deal of argument from both sides I got to my feet and recounted the true story of the Wellington pilot from 3 Group who lost his nerve over Essen and without a word to his crew, baled out of the top escape hatch and left them to it. The rear gunner and front gunner evidently thought this was no place for them and promptly followed suit leaving the navigator and wireless operator behind. The wireless operator was about to jump when the navigator called him back and announced that he was going to have a go at flying the aeroplane.

This was no mean task as the bombload was still aboard and the Wellington was in a spin but he managed to get himself in the pilot's seat, wrestled with the controls and somehow brought the aircraft on to an even keel. They jettisoned the bombs and set course for England, the wireless operator obtaining a fix. The only flying the navigator had done was a couple of hours in the Link Trainer so it was a very noble effort on his part.

They succeeded in bringing the Wellington back to England and the wireless operator was all for baling out there and then but the navigator argued that having got so far he was going to have a go at landing it. They found an aerodrome without much difficulty which turned out to be Bircham Newton and joined the circuit asking permission to land! They received a green Aldis lamp from the controller and the navigator joined the circuit and had a stab at landing. Quite understandably he made a complete mess of the approach, hit the runway hard with his wheels and ballooned high in the air; at the last moment he banged the throttles open and went round again.

Once again the wireless operator implored the navigator to bale out but again, quite naturally, the navigator was dead keen to complete the sortie and once more asked permission to land. This granted, he made another approach but the same thing happened again and he ballooned high into the air. On the third attempt they received a red Aldis lamp refusing permission, but undaunted the navigator pressed on, made the most ghastly landing on one wheel twenty yards off the runway whilst another aircraft was landing alongside (hence the red Aldis lamp) and finally came to rest in a dispersal point in one piece, and *very* relieved!

The duty flying control officer was livid at this rank disobedience, hopped in his motor car and drove round to the Wellington very irate. 'Where's the Captain of this aircraft?' he shouted and the two stalwarts had great pleasure in telling him.

As a result of this achievement the navigator was awarded the Conspicuous Gallantry Medal, an immediate commission in the field and an immediate pilot's course. It was a wonderful performance but sad to relate he was killed later as captain of an aircraft.

However, I made my point that the navigator was immediately given a pilot's course, and the motion was carried almost unanimously. Although it is very controversial I still firmly maintain that the pilot is best suited for captaincy as he is at the controls and is in a better position to make decisions quickly. There were many successful captains of aircraft – people like Wing Commander Nigel Bennett, a navigator, and Wing Commander Bevington, a navigator – but these were exceptions to the rule and generally I don't think it worked very well. It was usual and normal for a sergeant pilot to be captain of an aircraft where there were officers in the crew, but in the air in action against the enemy all ranks were as one, all contributing to the completion of an operation successfully.

Nigel Bennett, I believe, was the first navigator in 4 Group, Bomber Command, to become a squadron commander and he ran his squadron *most* efficiently, flying himself as navigator and captain on ops. He completed his second tour, was decorated and posted to HQ Bomber Command near High Wycombe as Command Navigation Officer to Bomber Harris. I need say no more about Nigel Bennett save to add that he held down this job under the RAF's most exacting taskmaster for a long while! Nigel is now a highly successful business man, (a chartered accountant by profession) and is happily married to Isobel in a lovely house at Pinkney's Green, near Maidenhead.

My old AOC 4 Group, Air Marshal Sir Roddy Carr, now lives at Bampton near Oxford and looks no older than the day he left No 4 Group in 1945. He was a good-looking New Zealander and had command of No 4 Group for 3½ years, longer than any other Group Commander in Bomber Command! He was a much loved commander, fair and efficient and it was his Group who turned out men like Group Captain Cheshire, Wing Commander Willie Tait, Squadron Leader Clayton, Wing Commander Calder – in fact half the Dambuster Squadron were 4 Group men! Young Clayton, who was my deputy flight commander at Rufforth, held the DSO, DFM and CGM (Conspicuous Gallantry Medal – other ranks' equivalent of the DSO) before he was twenty – a farmer's son from Yorkshire! Air Marshal Sir Roddy Carr's wife, Phyl, was my wife's second cousin.

We completed the commanders' course on 10th May and my ability as a potential commander was raised as 'Above Average'. The report stated: 'A sound and reliable officer of the best type. He has displayed great keenness and initiative throughout the course and should be an asset to any unit signed Air Commodore Hardy.' I returned to Rufforth where Group Captain Young wanted me appointed as Wing Commander Chief Flying Instructor, but a New Zealander, Bob Neal, got the job as he had a great friend at Group Headquarters who was able to use his influence. I was extremely lucky at not being sent back on operations, considering that I had now done fifteen months instructing.

Hank Iveson went back early in 1944 and was given command of No 76 Squadron at Holme-on-Spalding-Moor just near Market Weighton. He asked Group Captain Young for a good flight commander from Rufforth and he sent Squadron Leader Clack. Sad to say he was killed within a week. He then got Squadron Leader Somerscales and he went missing believed killed inside a month, and finally he got my old friend Squadron Leader Bickerdike and he too was killed on operations. It seemed to Hank Iveson as though he had a hoodoo at 76 Squadron and Group Captain Young was reluctant to part with any more flight commanders! I considered myself lucky in that during the period in later 1943 and early 1944 when the Hun defences were at their most vicious and night fighters were taking a heavy toll of bomber crews, I was in a safe seat flying instructing.

Although it was a different sort of 'fear' teaching young pilots to fly Halifaxes at night, it undoubtedly caused colossal strain without our knowing it and at the time, nearly being killed by a frightened pupil, I said I'd rather do another tour of ops than do this instructing. Not all our pupils were inexperienced – I had the honour of teaching a Commandant Ostree – a senior Air France pilot who'd flown 14,000 hours on air liners. I showed him *one* take-off and landing in a Halifax and he then changed seats with me and flew it better than I ever could! He later commanded the first all-French Squadron in 4 Group and was a very popular and competent squadron commander. They made us laugh, these 'Froggies' – if the target was in occupied France, their whole squadron would be stood down as someone had a popsie living in the French village and baulked at bombing it! We trained the complete French squadron at Rufforth and I met some marvellous pilots and charming Frenchmen. They did several sorties before they lost a Halifax and that one in tragic circumstances. Apparently on return from an 'op' on Berlin (which the French enjoyed!) one of their senior pilots landed back at base and unbeknown to anyone aboard they had a 1,000 lb. H.E. bomb hung up, fused! The slight shock of the landing caused it to explode and the aircraft and crew were blown to smithereens. They never found a complete body after the explosion! How horrible war was!

Frequently during this period Bomber Command was losing 10

and 15 per cent of the force dispatched and although one's second tour was only twenty operations, there were very few crews who completed a second tour before getting the chop! One must remember that the Germans in late 1943 and 1944 built up a fantastic radar network and their fighter controllers and night fighter pilots were a very efficient crowd. As I've mentioned before, their task was easy once they found the bomber stream and Ground Control was easy to follow and they took a frightful toll of bomber crews. They even copied our N/F techniques and sent night fighters back to England with the bombers, with the result that quite a few Lancasters and Halifaxes were shot down before they got back to base or even on their own circuit. To think that the German night fighter pilot Major Schnauffer bagged nine four-engined bombers (63 men) in one night over the Ruhr! Not one of our night or day fighter pilots could equal or surpass that fiendish performance.

CHAPTER VI

Number 100 Group

In September 1944 – almost eighteen months after my first tour of operations – I was sent for by Group Headquarters for an interview with the AOC of 100 Group in Norfolk with a view to my commanding a new squadron. Squadron Leader Gaskell from 4 Group was also selected and the choice lay between one of us two. I attended an interview with Air Vice-Marshal E.B. Addison at Dereham Hall in Norfolk and he announced that I had been selected and was to report as wing commander to North Creake (in North Norfolk) in charge of No 171 Squadron, on 28th September 1944.

I said goodbye to all my friends at Rufforth and set out in my little Austin Seven to motor to North Creake, wondering what sort of a place it was going to be and what the personnel on my squadron were like. It was different from taking over an existing squadron – this was an entirely new squadron, just formed, with new aircraft, new crews and new officers. North Creake lay inland about 3½ miles from Wells-next-the-Sea, and was more or less plumb in the middle of the Earl of Leicester's estate at Holkham. The area was pretty flat and ideal for an aerodrome.

I was introduced to Group Captain N.A.N. Bray, the Station Commander and Wing Commander Bevington who commanded the other squadron at North Creake – he was a navigator and in command of a squadron of Stirlings. Our work in 100 Group was of a secret nature and consisted entirely of spoofing the Hun defences and harrying his night fighter organisation.

The group was run entirely by fighter people and I knew from the start that my job was not going to be an easy one. Most of the squadrons in the group were Mosquito-equipped and there were only 171 and 199 Squadrons with Halifax Mk III's and Stirlings and 214 Squadron and Fortresses, which made up the heavy bomber units. To begin with I was allowed twenty new Halifaxes but these were all sent to St Athan to have special equipment fitted and so it was decided to give me one flight of Stirlings from 199 Squadron to get started. It wasn't until 21st October that I got my first two Halifax aircraft and I had to wait until the end of November before I got the lot. Meanwhile fourteen Halifax crews had been posted to me from 4 Group and, with few exceptions, I thought they were pretty awful. Evidently all squadrons in 4 Group had been asked to allocate one crew to 100 Group, 171 Squadron, and my guess was that this had enabled their squadron commanders to get rid of their unwanted garbage!

I promptly climbed in my aeroplane, flew up to York and demanded an interview with the AOC; when I saw him I put my cards on the table and said that I considered I had been sent a load of poor crews and asked him to personally make a few changes. He reluctantly agreed and certain crews were removed from my squadron and better replacements sent.

All this while I was trying to get my Halifaxes operational and my new crews trained to fly the new Halifax MkIII. These aircraft were fitted with Bristol Hercules radial engines and had a tremendous rate of climb and were a lot faster than Lancasters. Because of the new equipment modifications at St Athan I didn't operate for weeks myself and I certainly didn't fancy flying an old Stirling. Instead I amused myself in the evenings with trips to the local hostelries and such, and life for a few short weeks was very pleasant.

I met the Earl and Countess of Leicester on numerous occasions and they were a delightful and most hospitable couple and often invited me over to Holkham Hall for dinner. Our aerodrome was a haven for game and abounded in partridge and pheasants and I decided to use my rifle. Many was the evening when I'd go out in my Hillman car and shoot six brace of partridges and a couple of brace of pheasants. It wasn't exactly good sportsmanship but meat rationing was in force and I was determined that my parents should eat well – most of my other relations, uncles and aunts received many a brace of partridge through the post! I found, shooting from a car at about seventy yards range, that a covey of partridge would stay put and not fly and I remember on one occasion bagging the whole covey of twelve birds!

Pheasants were easier because they were much bigger targets and a very amusing incident occurred near Christmas. I was invited over to a sergeants' mess party one night and a sergeant armourer came up to me and told me that he'd been hiding in a hedge with a twelve bore gun trying to stalk a cock pheasant some seventy yards away. He crept up nearer to it and when he got within range he raised his gun and was about to fire when the cock pheasant suddenly fell on its back dead!

He neither saw nor heard anything and was very puzzled when suddenly he saw the new Squadron Commander running across the field to pick it up! Evidently I had stopped my car on the perimeter track and had taken a bead on his cock with my rifle and had fired just as the sergeant was taking aim! We laughed about it but I decided that I had better be more careful as I didn't want to be known as a poacher. The sergeant couldn't say anything because he had no business to be in possession of a station twelve bore!

I asked Air Vice-Marshal Carr for Squadron Leader Robertson from 4 Group and he very kindly agreed to post him in – Robbie was a very good type and I'd had him at Rufforth. My other flight commander was Squadron Leader Riches but he was a Stirling pilot and near the end of his second tour. By now the Halifaxes were nearly completed and I looked like getting operational and back into harness. The thought didn't exactly please me but I had not flown in action since September and was fairly free from fear at the moment.

Our aircraft was equipped with about forty wireless transmitters for jamming purposes and we formed what was known as a 'Mandrel' screen across the entry to enemy territory. This screen effectively jammed all the Hun radio frequencies with the result that the bomber stream was able to fly through the screen and they wouldn't be plotted by the enemy until they were actually over enemy or enemy-occupied territory. Until 100 Group started operations the bomber stream was plotted over England soon after take-off and the Hun, by radar, was able to plot the course of the bombers and guess fairly accurately which was to be the target. In those days of late 1943 and early 1944 the technique of dummy thrusts and attacking more than one target was unheard of and the Hun was taking a very heavy toll.

Our Halifaxes were also modified to take 'window' – (strips of silver paper, which, when dropped from an aircraft, looked like a bomber stream on the enemy radar screen) and there was a chute fitted so that the operator could throw out tons of 'window' at a given signal. This chucking out of 'window' was more difficult than it sounds – it involved the wireless operator heaving out literally a ton of paper in 28 lb packets – no mean feat in the bitter cold of the fuselage and at oxygen height! We knew from our Intelligence service in Europe that these tactics were very successful and quite often the Hun mistakenly plotted two or three Halifaxes dropping 'window' as a major force approaching a target and diverted his night fighters to the assumed route. For this reason the work was dangerous and my few aircraft often were set upon by night fighters since they only numbered half a dozen or so.

During early December I met the Earl of Leicester's two daughters, Lady Silvia Combe and Lady Mary Harvey, both of whom were very attractive and charming girls. So too was Elizabeth Coke, the wife of the Earl of Leicester's son, Thomas Coke. They were all most hospitable to Bray, Bevington and me and we went to endless parties at their home. Silvia and Mary were sweet girls and I used to take them to a lot of dances – they were such good fun and such good company. Lord Leicester was unbelievably hospitable and being passionately fond of music he used to invite me to Holkham Hall to listen to private recitals by Solomon and Tertis, the well-known viola player. The Hall itself was a magnificent building and in the entrance hall were three marvellous paintings by Rubens, Gainsborough and Van Dyck.

It was difficult for us to return their excellent hospitality because our mess food was appalling, (there seemed an unending supply of corned beef) but I nonetheless suggested to Group Captain Bray that we invite the Earl and Countess in to dinner in the mess.

He thought it a good idea but said: 'What can we give them to eat?'

I suggested a nice brace of pheasants and he said: 'Marvellous! But where can we get hold of pheasants?'

I told him that I had a rifle and that I'd go out and poach a brace and he was horrified.

He said, 'We can't give Lord Leicester a brace of his own

pheasants for dinner.' But I argued that he wouldn't know where they came from.

He reluctantly agreed. So I went in my Hillman for a race round the aerodrome boundary with my rifle across my lap. I had no success, although I saw plenty of partridges, until I went round the bomb dump. This was at the farthest point from the aerodrome buildings and I saw a lovely brace of pheasants just crouched by a hedge. Bang bang, and inside half a minute I was back to the mess with a brace of beautiful young pheasants! I showed them to Bray who nearly had kittens and we hung them up in my quarters for a week, and Bray duly invited the Earl and Countess to dinner and the four of us sat down to a glorious meal; the chef had done bread sauce, game chips, bacon and all the trimmings and we'd scrounged some tinned fruit salad and some cheese to follow. We bought a bottle of wine at the local pub and altogether we put on a fine banquet for our charming visitors.

Halfway through the meal Lord Leicester, with a twinkle in his eye, said, 'Remarkably devoid of shot these birds, Michael!' I nearly collapsed but laughed later at the thought that he knew he was eating his own birds, each with a small hole drilled neatly by a .22 bullet.

One night I took Silvia and Mary over to a mess dance some thirty miles from North Creake at Little Snoring and on the way back the Hillman sustained two punctures at Fakenham. I had to ring up the duty officer at two o'clock in the morning for another car and he wasn't very pleased to be got out of bed, but I just couldn't be stranded miles from home with two beautiful members of the aristocracy. I remember the three of us sitting on a bench in Fakenham market square singing RAF songs and waiting for our car to be sent out! Silvia was married to Simon Combe the brewer and Mary to a Captain in the army – Elizabeth's husband Tom Leicester was also away at the war and practically every night that December I was invited to one or the other of their houses. Silvia lived in a glorious house in Burnham Thorpe and used to give marvellous dinner parties, so did Elizabeth who lived not far from Holkham Hall. I could never wish to meet three more charming people and their hospitality to us at North Creake was out of this world.

One day I had a fright when I read in the newspaper that a baronet had been found dead in a field next to the aerodrome with a .22 bullet through his head. I immediately imagined that one of my poaching shots had ricocheted and killed him. I felt awful and couldn't confide in a soul about this awful accident. Everything pointed to my guilt; I had been poaching along the road by this field and had fired at a lovely cock pheasant but missed at 100 yards and had then hit him with my second. I raced across the field and retrieved my pheasant and arrived back at my quarters breathless. Imagine, next morning, when this baronet's death was announced I thought I was in for a manslaughter charge. The following day the papers carried the story that Sir Blank had been killed accidentally in a 'shooting incident'. I was reprieved! I knew the dangers in using my Remington .22 rifle and the cartridge packet was marked: 'Caution. Dangerous within 1 mile'.

I was elected President of the Mess Committee at North Creake and Group Captain Bray and I decided to hold a fabulous party in the mess. We flew a Halifax over to France and brought back fresh lobsters and champagne and I organised one room in the mess to be a miniature casino! We discovered that someone in the airmen's mess had been a professional croupier in peace-time so we got hold of him and put him in evening dress and made him in charge of the gambling department! Bray and I thought that we'd make enough on the roulette table to pay for the party (about £600) but we hadn't reckoned on this so-called croupier; as the evening wore on he accepted drinks right and left and finished up tight as a coot paying everybody and falling off the back of his stool. He was a dead loss and cost us money.

Silvia Combe drove over in her car and joined in the party and after it was all over I saw her to her car which wasn't there! She was most upset as there had been illicit use of petrol and she saw herself headlined in the *Daily Mirror* and the *News of the World*. However, after a very thorough search we found the car, which had been 'borrowed' by a drunken airman and all was well.

The party was a great success but so it should have been considering the cost. I remember Squadron Leader Robertson getting somewhat whistled half way through the evening and he was standing with a plate of cold lobster and salad while I cut up a daffodil stalk into his salad. He ate everything without a murmur!

Although living out was strictly against the rules I managed to get Yvonne up before Christmas and she stayed at the little pub, the Crown, at Wells, for about three months. The Kitsons, cockneys from East London, ran the place and they were most kind and generous to Yvonne. When I wasn't operating or in charge of night flying operations I used to go over and visit her and spend the night there if there was nothing doing at North Creake. We had a simple code: I used to ring her up and say that I was 'busy' (that meant that my squadron were operating but that I wasn't flying myself) but if I said that I was 'very, very busy' that meant that I was flying on operations myself and she would know not to expect me back until the early hours of the morning.

She used to count the aircraft in the circuit when we returned to base, as many anxious wives have done, but it was such an unreliable method of assessing losses that I persuaded her to give up the idea and sleep. This silly business of counting the returning bombers on the circuit was entirely unreliable. You could count thirty aircraft take off but landing was different as some planes circuited three or four times before landing owing to the congestion in the air above of twenty-five returning bombers.

Christmas came and we had lots of parties and because of bad weather flying was very restricted. The squadron was now operating efficiently and I had got a good crowd of officers and aircrew under me and I felt fairly confident. On Boxing Day morning Simon Combe and Silvia invited me over to cold turkey and to shoot wildfowl afterwards down on Holkham marshes. What a glorious day we had; it was misty and cold down on the marshes and we didn't shoot many duck but I was full of turkey and Christmas pudding and in very charming company so I couldn't have cared less.

On 28th December 1944 I did my first operation of my second tour and was part of a Mandrel screen on the German border. All the old fears came crowding in by now, only this time instead of being a bachelor as I was on my first tour, I was now desperately in love, a married man, and I cared very greatly whether I would die or survive. Being the Squadron Commander carried heavy responsibilities alone – but now I had so much more to lose. I hated every minute of my second tour and thanks to God (and the atom bomb) I only completed ten operations out of my twenty when the war ended. Yvonne would insist on being near at hand during this period but that caused me additional worry as it was against the regulations on an operational tour of duty to live with one's wife (or even one's mistress!).

I used to sneak into our bedroom at the Crown Hotel in Wells often at 4 a.m. after an op and we would hold one another tight at being reunited after risking death on operations. We lived a sort of married life at odd hours of the day and night and little wonder that Yvonne was emotionally upset.

I had a very good navigator in Flight Sergeant Bates but the rest of the crew were drawn from the pool and we had a singularly uneventful trip. After taking up our station we had to orbit for something like three and a half hours and it was a very tedious business and one had to be constantly on the look out for fighters and other aircraft and the eye strain was considerable. A station was made up of two aircraft and these flew at slightly different heights on the same orbit. If one aircraft had to return to base for some reason then a replacement was dispatched with all possible speed since it took always two aircraft to jam sufficient of the Hun frequencies. Strictly speaking one was not supposed to leave the Mandrel station until a replacement bomber took over. The screen itself was probably composed of thirty aircraft from our two squadrons, using both Stirlings and Halifaxes.

This job of ours was reasonably safe and I can't honestly say that I was as frightened as I had been on any of my trips on the first tour. After this the weather clamped down and I didn't operate until towards the end of January.

I had an airman corporal clerk on the unit, who was a fly merchant and had been in the motor trade before the war, he was in all the fiddles that he could be. He ran a Rover 1935 'Speed Fourteen' saloon which I bought from him for £180. I sold my Austin, which had cost me £35, for £50 to an Australian pilot and I was now the proud owner of a Rover. I was not strictly allowed to use my RAF Hillman for leave or for gadding about on pleasure jaunts and the old Rover came in very useful. Yvonne was now expecting our first child which was due in June, so I had to pack her off home, but not before she caught mumps at Wells! She was swelling literally everywhere, poor girl, and went through a lot that winter at North Creake. She used to come during the day and serve in the NAAFI canteen lorry on the aerodrome and she became very popular with the squadron and ground crews. She didn't know one end of an aeroplane from the other but we showed her over a Stirling and a Halifax and she began to see the other side of our lives.

As Squadron Commander I didn't want to pick my operations for fear that I might select the easy targets and be criticised for it, so I used to tell my Adjutant that I would fly on such a date on operations and take pot luck with the target. If it was a tough or an easy one, at least I hadn't selected it. My fears began to build up again and I had so much more to lose now with an attractive wife whom I adored and a child on the way. I simply hated the thought of flying on operations over Germany but there was no one I could turn to and I had to bottle up my fears like everyone else. I wanted to discuss my feelings with someone but one was lonely and comparatively aloof as a squadron commander and the last thing was to show that one had nerves. As a squadron commander I missed the chatter and leg-pulling in the locker room before an op – I had to change in my office on the edge of the perimeter track and it was there, in complete privacy, that I was able to get into my long combs! I used to dislike being alone with my thoughts and I used to change pretty quickly (after the Lord's prayer) and get out to join my crews.

During February I carried out three Mandrel operations and apart from a good deal of flak near the heavily bombarded targets I was comparatively fear-free. However 100 Group now had the idea that we should carry bombs as well as 'window' and this was going to make our task more hazardous. In other words the main bomber stream were to come through the screen at one point and we were to act as a diversion numbering only a dozen aircraft to some target like Stuttgart. This was bound to draw the night fighters and I knew that my squadron losses were going to increase. To date I had only lost a handful of crews and morale on the squadron was high – replacements were arriving steadily but not at a pace, thank God, and we were a very happy and a fairly efficient unit.

Our Senior Air Staff Officer, Rory Chisholm, and our Group Wing Commander Flying, Wing Commander Dunning White, were both ex-fighter boys and they hadn't got much of a clue when it came to knowing about bombing-up a Halifax. They were inclined to change the bombload half an hour before take-off and wonder why it took so long! The fighter outlook was permanently present and they regarded the Halifax much as a Mosquito when it came to refuelling and bombing-up. Little Bray was a man of intense energy and he certainly kept me busy as a squadron commander, what with training and conferences and visits to Group Headquarters. He lived out with his wife and children at a village called Little Walsingham and many was the time when my wife and I were invited there to dinner with the Leicesters. Little 'Nan' Bray, as we called him (his initials were N.A.N.) was a ball of fire, not frightfully competent as a station commander, but had *everyone* 'organised'. He couldn't have been more than 5 feet 4 inches tall but he was like a human dynamo and worked me to the bone. It was he, and I'll never forget it, who recalled me from 7 days' leave to tell me he thought I should be with my squadron and not on leave! He said he felt sure that the war was about to end (April 1945 and I should be leading my squadron into battle! Accordingly I did three trips to Kiel, Berlin and Potsdam in quick succession, but it was 'Nan' who put me up for the American DFC as a result of a slight contretemps with three night fighters over Berlin!

It was he, at the end of the war, who organised the biggest parade of aircrew and groundcrew ever seen at North Creake on the disbandment of my 171 Squadron. He invited the AOC, all the VIP's for miles around, the Bishop of Norwich, the Leicesters, in fact, I recall, half of Norfolk! The parade went with a swing but it was pure 'bull' and the speeches went on for hours. I was stuck out there in front, dressed in my Moss Bros best and the awful 'cheesecutter' that I hated, whilst 'Nan' said, 'This Squadron was formed only in Spetember 1944, became an efficient unit only to be disbanded in June 1945'! What a tragedy,' he added. It was Nan who held the most lavish and riotous parties in the mess at North Creake and always invited the local VIP's – it was he who organised a miniature casino so that our winnings would pay the bill. (If it hadn't been for the drunken croupier, I believe they would!)

My tailwheel jammed sideways on one occasion as I taxied out from dispersal and I couldn't steer the Halifax. I should have stopped and tried to let my fitters fix it but I knew that meant a half hour's delay and I was supposed to lead my squadron, not follow them, so we pressed on towards the runway, skidding in all directions in thick snow! I had a hell of a job to line up on the runway and I knew it was a risk with a full bombload and petrol load and all the radio jamming equipment, but I thought if I could get the tail up quickly off the snow, we'd make it. Actually it took me the whole runway, skidding and braking before I could haul the Halifax off the ground.

One of the jobs I hated most was writing a letter to bereaved parents and wives when aircraft and crews went missing. I realised how my mother would have felt had she received the fateful letter which always begin: 'It is with the deepest regret that I have to inform you that your son P/O Smith is missing believed killed as a result of air operations on the night of February 22nd . . . ' I used to write the letters personally whenever I could, but each aircraft meant eight letters and one just hadn't the time to sit and write them all freehand. I hated typewritten letters but on occasions I had no alternative.

What was worse was when a wife was living close by the aerodrome and that meant a visit. I recall one occasion when at four o'clock in the morning I went to call on a young wife to tell her that her husband had been killed in a crash. The little cottage was tucked away in the country and when I knocked on the door and this sweet girl of twenty-two came to answer the bell; as soon as she saw me she guessed what I had come to say. I took her inside and made a pot of tea but the poor girl was so shocked that she couldn't speak and walked from the kitchen to the lounge in a dream.

My heart bled for this newly-married wife and I felt on the verge of tears myself, but what could I do? I couldn't bring her husband and lover back to life – he was a hulk of charred flesh lying silently in the mortuary and no words of mine could comfort her. I remember I stayed with her till 7 a.m. just sitting holding her hand. I was only twenty-four myself and though I felt a hardened campaigner who had been through all this many times before, yet each occasion seemed worse than the last.

I never really got used to death although one naturally became very callous and hardened to it. One only had to think of one's own wife and how she would react to the receipt of the fateful letter and telegram for it to be stark reality. God, how I hated the war. Death came quickly and violently to bomber crews but for those they left behind all the sadness lingered on. Shall I ever forget those awful days of the war and being petrified every time one flew? It must have taken a peculiar kind of courage to hide one's fears and to keep it all bottled up – played utter hell with one's nerves.

One strange phenomenon we discovered quite by chance on a Mandrel operation in March. Whilst orbiting in the Mandrel screen we saw a glare of light 15,000 feet below in Germany and suddenly this bright light started slowly to come up and passed us at a colossal speed. They were the V2 rockets, and five minutes later we could actually see them explode in the London area. We used to report the exact position of the launching sites by radio and a special force of 5 Group bombers would come next day and destroy the concrete ramp from which they were launched. Later the Germans used mobile launching points and our coded messages were of no avail. What ghastly weapons they were! But thank God, owing to the successful raid on Peenemünde and to 5 Group's bombing of the launching pads, London only got a fraction of the V weapons that were planned to be despatched.

I recall one dirty night at North Creake in March 1945, whilst we were waiting for our squadron's return from a raid, hearing an aircraft approaching the aerodrome. The aerodrome control pilot came on the R/T and announced that an aircraft on fire was approaching to land. I gave instructions for the aerodrome and flarepath lighting to be switched on immediately, and we came out on the balcony of the flying control tower to see the trouble. We could hear this full-throated roar of an aircraft approaching when suddenly it appeared over the aerodrome and we could see that it was a V1 flying bomb. We all dived for shelter, but it soon became apparent that its engine was not going to cut out and we stood and watched; the ghastly thing came down near King's Lynn.

This was shortly followed by several more, and Group Headquarters were on the phone from Dereham warning us that flying bombs were coming in over Norfolk in large numbers. In fact seventeen of them came in over the coast of Norfolk that night and one fell so close to Group HQ that the ceiling came down in the operations room! These were the only flying bombs I ever saw but one was enough, and I felt for the people in London and south-east England. Funnily enough these V1's were meant for London and were launched from Heinkel 111's over the North Sea, but because of a strong northerly gale the aircraft were miles off course and so as a result, were the V1's.

On 14th April I briefed my crews for operations on Berlin and the main force were to attack a target close at hand. We carried bombs this time and about two tons of 'window' so it looked like being a warm trip. I cannot express the thoughts that went through my mind that night. This was to be our first trip with bombs and Berlin was very heavily defended we knew. I was badly coned over the city and we were attacked by three separate night fighters in the target area.

My mid-upper gunner, Sergeant Feasy, wrote about that night: 'I can remember quite well the trip on 14th April 1945, which was most exciting. The crew were Flight Sergeant 'Rusty' Willis – wireless operator, Flight Sergeant McDonald special wireless operator to throw out the 'window', Flying Officer James, a newly commissioned Canadian who was rear gunner, and myself, mid-upper. Shortly after take-off which was at 18.35 hours, the rear gunner's intercom went u/s, after which we heard nothing from him until our return to base. We carried 5,750 lb. incendiary clusters and HE, with the rest of the load and made up of 'window'.

'The trip to Berlin was uneventful – I think the engineer, Wireless Operator Gold, saw what looked like a fighter some distance off which didn't interfere. On reaching Potsdam which was about the spot where we dropped our load, we were suddenly coned by about six searchlights; several more immediately caught on until we must have had sixteen or more on us. I think we were all practically blinded but it was then that I think an Me410 was sighted on the port beam. You were weaving violently and I remember calling to you to corkscrew. The fighter opened fire on us from quite a distance and the cannon fire passed over the top of us. I can remember calling over the intercom to you to dive first port and then up starboard, thinking that I could see the lights from a better position than you, thereby getting in a more favourable spot.

'We were coned for thirteen minutes altogether and you were weaving and diving all the time, in fact you were breathing and puffing hard from exertion. We then had another attack from the starboard side by a Ju88 which I personally didn't see until the cannon fire went under the starboard wing. It was after this that you made a masterly move. You were at the top of a climb when you saw a fighter apparently making a head-on attack. This must have been the FW190. At the moment of seeing the aircraft, I remember you telling us that you kicked the rudder or did some yawing movement which made our Halifax yaw sideways at the exact moment the fighter opened fire on us. The cannon shells went under the port wing.

'This was confirmed by Rusty Willis afterwards who laughingly told us that he was itching to see what was going on outside his w/op's cabin and at the moment he pulled back his little side curtain he was in time to see the cannon shells go screaming past his side window. He hurriedly pulled the curtain closed again! Miraculously we were not hit in any of these attacks.

'I always remember calling out to you, "Up starboard, dive to port" hoping that it'd help. I often wondered afterwards why you never told me to shut up, but I felt quite exhilarated. It was all this weaving which I believe made us short of fuel. I fired my guns once during this period at a fighter which was way up above; I remember this because I could only just elevate them sufficiently to get a sight. My fire, of course, went nowhere near. After that I think we just flew out of the searchlight belt and made for home.'

Several times during that encounter I felt sure I was going to be shot down and I thought of my poor darling Yvonne hearing the news that we were 'missing believed killed'. My mouth went dry at the first attack and I literally felt my hair standing on end during the excitement in the target area. The strange thing was that although I was scared out of my wits, I managed to remain calm and hoped that my skill as a bomber pilot would out-manoeuvre the comparatively inexperienced night fighter pilots on my tail.

No one who hasn't been through this sort of night raid can possibly know what went on in one's mind – it was a mixture of jumbled thoughts, fears, apprehension and sheer terror all rolled into one. One felt so naked and exposed when coned by searchlights and it was as though one was on a stage with the arc lamps upon one. No amount of twisting and turning could rid one of the searchlights; they passed one on mile after mile and minutes seemed like years.

I had innumerable fears as a bomber pilot but none so horrific as those of attacks by night fighters. It was the knowledge that one was immediately at a disadvantage that frightened one. The more skilled and experienced night fighter pilots would press home their attacks ruthlessly and in the face of strong opposition from the rear and mid-upper gun turrets, and I think I was lucky throughout that my many attacks by night fighters were not those of expert or experienced men. Maybe they were and maybe my violent evasive action was enough to send them in search of a easier victim – I shall never know. All I remember is that nothing in life has frightened me more, and when one has lived through that sort of terror one could surely live through anything. The fact that it was never spoken about in the Mess was significant – men faced up to this fear and were always ready to go out and meet it. Death was just around the corner and one almost got used to it.

To be in command of an aircraft which was a mass of petrol tanks and bombs was very unnerving and my loathing and terror of fire was always uppermost in my thoughts. Petrol went up like a bomb and one was so quickly burnt. I remember one of my pilots at North Creake, Flight Lieutenant Butler, crashing on take-off and the aircraft exploded just near a hangar. Butler opened the top hatch and jumped out but he was covered in burning petrol in seconds before anyone could reach him and pull him to safety. It is doubtful whether Butler was alight for more than five seconds at the outside, but when I visited him in hospital in the burns ward at Cambridge, his face was almost unrecognisable. He had skin grafting later for new eyelids, new nose and eye-brows. It amazed me, who had been present at the scene of the crash, that the burns could have affected him so much.

There was nothing more sickening than the sight of a burning aircraft and that pall of jet black smoke which one always associated with a crash. The thought of fire was always with me and I dreaded it happening to me or my crew. I used to suffer the awful nightmare of being set on fire over Germany and used to wake up my Yvonne by yelling at the top of my voice! Other than that I slept like a baby.

We lived a very false and hollow life as a result of operational flying, and the tendency was to throw mad mess parties and pub crawls. The spirit of a fellowship amongst men was one fine thing that existed in the face of a common danger. Operational aircrew knew very well that the next trip might be the last and to live a normal life with such knowledge was virtually impossible. I knew I would miss this fellowship in peace-time (if I survived) and I decided to try and become a Freemason. This wasn't difficult and my friend Ernest Sugden was going to propose me for membership for his Lodge in Howden, Yorks. However, as I'd probably settle in the South of England he advised me at the last minute to join a lodge where I was to live – my 'Mother Lodge'. In fact I never became a Mason as I would really have wanted to be with Ernest Sugden.

In March I lost a very nice crew, the pilot of which was Flight Lieutenant Stone. He was married to a sweet girl and I had been to the wedding only a few weeks before. I got my adjutant to write the usual letters to the parents of the other crew members but I wrote personally to Mrs Stone. I did something in that letter which I'd never done before and which was not really sensible; I told her that there was every chance that her young husband had baled out and might be safe in enemy hands. I did this because I knew that she would take the phrase 'Missing believed killed' very badly and although I was sticking my neck out I felt it was worth the risk with so sweet a girl. Luck must have been on my side for a few weeks later Stone was reported a prisoner of war in Germany and I joyously wrote to Mrs Stone again telling her the marvellous news.

She came over to see me at the aerodrome and I took her out to lunch in Wells and within four weeks the Russians had liberated a number of prisoners and Flight Lieutenant Stone was repatriated. He and his young wife came to see me again at North Creake and he looked perfectly fit except for a shaven head!

He told me the usual story – that they had been coned in searchlights near Berlin and a burst of cannon fire from nowhere exploded a petrol tank on the starboard wing. In seconds the whole of the starboard was a mass of roaring flames and he gave the order urgently to bale out. They all abandoned the aircraft safely and whilst Stone was drifting down at the end of his parachute he saw the Halifax, still coned in searchlights, start to disintegrate, and explode on the ground below, only 500 yards from where he parachuted down. He was taken to the central questioning depot at Frankfurt and after a week was moved to a Stalagluft near the Baltic where he was later released by the Russians.

All aircrew shot down *anywhere* in Europe were first taken to the Central German Interrogation centre at Frankfurt-am-Main. Here they asked you lots of questions, some of them cleverly disguised or suggestive, but all you were required to give was Name, Rank and Number. Those who were kept there longer than a day or two could reckon they were being useful to the Hun! Otherwise you were immediately moved to a prisoner of war camp (*Stalagluft* for aircrew) The Germans were very wily and used all sorts of ruses and subterfuges. Their Intelligence kept copies of all British newspapers and a 'dossier' was kept on anyone mentioned in Engagements, Births, Marriages, headlines of famous pilots, exploits, decorations – the lot, in a typically German thorough way. Imagine your consternation if the interrogator suddenly said: 'How are Yvonne and Alan?' Your immediate reaction (not knowing that they'd seen the press announcements) was 'How the hell did they know?' and the Interrogator would say, 'Oh! It's all right, your navigator told us and also what squadron you're with and lots more.' So your unguarded reaction was – 'Well, what's the use of staying silent if Tim Collins has blown the gaff.'

Many were quite naturally fooled by this and gave the Hun a lot of information. We used similar dodges in England and the favourite trick during the Battle of Britain was to get hold of an unconscious fighter pilot or bomber pilot (Hun) and rush him to a special hospital ward where they had German-speaking nurses and doctors and photos of Hitler on the wall and swastikas – the lot. When the Hun pilot came round and said, 'Where am I?' the answer was, 'It's all right you're safely back in *der Vaterland*!' (All in German this!) The reaction, dazed and bewildered, was to say, 'Thank *Gott* – I tought I vos in England!' and from then on it was easy.

This clever sort of interrogation worked well and so did other ways of spoofing the Hun. In 100 Group HQ we had an Austrian woman standing by a radio transmitter and a German-speaking Intelligence officer and used to transmit verbal instructions to German night fighters attacking our bomber stream over Germany. They told the fighters: 'Proceed immediately to intercept Bomber stream heading for Bremen.' This was quickly followed by a Hun controller's voice saying: 'Ignore that order, it vos ze *Engländer*!' The woman was on duty every night we, or Bomber Command, flew, simply in case the Germans used a woman controller – a thing they had never done, but which we expected them to do – and they did, to fool us! We were ready and our Austrian woman gave immediate counter-instructions which caused chaos over Germany!

The Germans were forced to give up 'plain language' control and had in 1945 to resort to playing certain music to indicate Bomber Command's target – we were on to that one too and in the end their night fighter control system was completely buggered! It thus saved hundreds of our aircrew and aircraft and we made the Hun night fighter's life even more unbearable by sitting Mosquitos all over their fighter aerodromes to shoot them down when they got back from their attacks! In 100 Group we spoofed them so thoroughly that no confidence existed at all in their defence system – it was brought to utter chaos and immediately our bomber losses were halved.

Stone was lucky to have been shot down so near the end of the war; other luckless aircrew who had been shot down in 1941 and 1942 spent a very long time in 'the bag'. Another friend of mine, ex-Rufforth, Flight Lieutenant Woodhatch, had been shot down by a fighter on a daylight raid on the Ruhr – the cannon shells punched holes in the main spar and the aircraft had broken in two, burning fiercely. Woodhatch was left alone in the nose which was spiralling earthwards but luckily he had time before the aircraft broke in two to put on his parachute. The centrifugal force of the spinning nose section kept Woodhatch firmly in the pilot's seat and he hadn't sufficient strength to lever himself out of it. The aircraft had fallen several thousand feet when, with a superhuman effort, he got down to the front escape hatch, pulled the parachute ripcord whilst still in the aircraft and it luckily billowed out in the slipstream and pulled him clear, only smashing both his kneecaps. He only dropped for a few seconds so the aircraft must have been at about 2,000 feet when he escaped, and landed in a garden on the outskirts of Essen. A chap came out of the house, helped Woodhatch to sit on the crossbar of his bicycle, and rode furiously down the road, Woodhatch was very elated although in agony and imagined he was being ridden to safety behind our lines but instead of which he was deposited outside the local police station! The German defences right up to the end of the war were venomous and they still had a very active night fighter force, not to mention the flak and searchlight concentrations, despite the fact that only a very small part of Germany remained unoccupied.

By the end of April we all knew that the end of the war was in sight and I was determined to take part in the last raids over enemy territory. This wasn't really fair on Yvonne as I was risking my life unnecessarily, but there was in me a strange excitement and a compulsion to fly on operations despite my hatred of it. I think it was explained by the fact that the war was to end in a matter of days and we all suffered from perhaps a little too-much confidence. I certainly did and it was nearly to be my undoing.

On 2nd May 1945 I briefed my crews for an attack on Kiel and we invited Lord Leicester and his wife and Mary Harvey and Silvia Combe to come over to the aerodrome to watch the take-off of a 'Maximum Effort'. (Strictly against the rules to have civilians present!) I remember I was lined up on the runway as the first aircraft to take off when suddenly, as I opened my throttles, I saw a private car driving down the runway towards us! I immediately closed down the power and waited as the car turned off towards the control tower. It turned out to be Mary Harvey who had got herself lost on the perimeter track and had mistakenly driven straight down the main runway. We pulled her leg about it afterwards but she might have been involved in a horrible accident; she said afterwards that she never saw the Halifax taking off!

Knowing this was to be more than likely the last operation of the war I took an entirely new crew with me, except for Flying Officer Bates, my navigator. I thought it would be nice for newly trained aircrew who hadn't done an operation to have the experience and excitement of a raid for the last time. Thank God in many ways that I did this, for it probably saved my life! We were attacked over Kiel by a Ju88 and I had great difficulty in shaking him off. Twice he attacked and twice I weaved out of his cannon fire but this was a tough fighter pilot and he wasn't put off. Trust my luck, I thought, to get shot down and killed within sight of VE Day! I eventually managed to get out of range of the searchlights and the next time the Ju88 attacked he hadn't the advantage of seeing me brightly coned in the sky and he missed us by yards. However, it wasn't the pleasantest sight to see red cannon shells streaming across one's nose. Both my mid-upper and rear gunners were firing at him but the Hun pilot was persistent and was as determined as I was.

We eventually shook him off and set course for home having dropped our 'window' and bombload over Kiel – the actual main force target was Berlin some distance away. At last I felt relaxed and the fear whilst being attacked was gone – I joked with the crew as we sped home across the North Sea and when we were about seventy miles off the Danish coast I suggested that we drank our coffee. I put 'George' in and was happily sipping my coffee when suddenly the rear gunner screamed at the top of his voice, 'Enemy fighter coming in astern'. I dropped my thermos flask, spilling coffee everywhere in the panic, pulled out the automatic pilot and thrust the control column forward in a sudden dive. As luck would have it, his first burst of cannon fire went right over the top of us but it was a near thing. His second burst caught us all along the fuselage and holes were punched in my old Halifax. I was virtually panic-stricken at being caught napping and loathed the thought of being shot down into the North Sea miles from land, so I flung the Halifax about desperately and dived down to sea level in an attempt to shake the Ju88 off. We eventually lost him and all breathed again!

There is no doubt, looking back, that this Hun was the Ju88 who had attacked us over the target area and he had cunningly followed us at a safe distance right out over the North Sea hoping to catch us unawares. Thanks to keen-eyed gunners who were obviously wide awake and excited, they spotted the attack in time. I wondered what would have happened if I'd had my old seasoned gunners with me – they would probably have been drinking coffee and smoking, feeling safe at having left the target area behind. There was a tendency amongst rear gunners to smoke from sheer boredom or tedium or nerves and I made it quite clear to my crew that if I caught them at it I'd have them court-martialled. But the glow of cigarette ends in the rear turret could be seen by a night fighter several hundred yards away on a dark night and seven or eight lives were at stake.

The shock of the rear gunner's scream nearly frightened me to death and I think that incident shook me more than any other. To be peacefully crossing the lonely North Sea and to be suddenly attacked like that was a frightful shock and I didn't feel either relaxed or comfortable until we landed at base.

Some weeks earlier one of my crews had been flying home over Cambridgeshire with the automatic pilot in when a night fighter intruder had attacked them. The Halifax burst into flames and the crew all baled out at about 1,000 feet and were lucky to have all survived. The wireless operator landed in a cemetery, poor chap, it seemed as though he was present at his own internment! One could never really relax on sorties at night; there was always the risk of collision, attacks by fighters and bombardment by flak. It didn't pay to relax one's concentration in the least and anyone who hasn't flown in action can never know the colossal mental strain of seven or eight hours in the night sky over a heavily defended Europe. The pilot and gunners were constantly straining their eyes in an endeavour to spot the vicious night fighter and that alone was a strain without attack of any sort. The question of who saw who first was vital and in nine cases out of ten the night fighter who was not spotted first would bag his victim as easily as the drop of a hat.

I was present at the interrogation of a famous Hun night fighter pilot who was brought down to our Group HQ in Norfolk just before the end of the war and he said his task was easy! I believe his name was Major Schnauffer – he was informed by German controllers where the bomber stream was heading and all he had to do was to rendezvous along the route and he had up to a thousand bombers to choose from. In addition to this he had airborne radar aids to interception, but mostly on a clear night his task was visual and dead easy. This was a man who had shot down nine four-engined bombers in one night and he was highly skilled! He made it quite clear to us that he carefully selected his victim from below and behind and if the bomber started corkscrewing or weaving before the attack, he would sheer off and find another victim. He swears that nearly every victim of his 127 victories was unaware of his presence and one long burst into the fuel tanks was curtains for the bomber. His 127 victories were confirmed – all four-engined bombers. The only real risk he faced was one of collision, because 1,000 bombers and night fighters all packed into an attack on a target in 30 minutes was a very considerable concentration and whilst the ground defences may have been swamped the task of the night fighter was a piece of cake.

Despite the work of 100 Group and the utter disorganisation of the German defences, the night fighters were full of guts to the last, as my operation on Kiel proved. One has only to visit the RAF memorial at Runnymede to see sixty thousand names of aircrew and others who completely disappeared and had no known grave! Sixty thousand men is a high figure, but to be destroyed in a bomber at 18,000 feet meant that very little would be found of the wreckage and this might be found scattered over a very wide area. Thousands of aircraft and crews must have been destroyed over the North Sea and several bombers trying to limp home after attack went down in the cold sea and were lost without trace.

Although we all wore identity discs round our necks, in the event of explosion or fire, the enemy would have had a job to identify seven shattered and incinerated bodies spread about a field. Even a four-engined bomber left very little trace after it had crashed from 18,000 feet and burnt out on the ground. Ditching a bomber in the North Sea was a hazardous business and 'curtains' if the sea was rough. On a calm sea, one landed wheels up at low speed but at night it was frightfully difficult to gauge one's height above water. The impact was like hitting a brick wall at 85 mph but if you were strapped in or braced for the shock, you were probably OK. The dinghy would automatically inflate (it was in the port wing panel) and was connected by rope to the bomber so you had to be a bit smartish to cut it adrift before the bomber sank! Anything from thirty seconds to one hour. Of course, you may have had some flak burst and shrapnel punctured the rubber, in which case your dinghy sank too – 'curtains' again!

CHAPTER SEVEN

Peace

On 8th May 1945 I was quietly shooting pigeons from a hide on
Lord Leicester's ground (with permission!) when one of my officers
came running over to me and told me that Winston Churchill had
just announced the end of hostilities on the wireless. I cannot
express the utter relief of this news, that I had survived the war in
one piece! I thought of all my friends and acquaintances who had
died over the years and I counted myself very fortunate that I had
lived through the horror of night bomber operations without a
scratch. Had there been some guiding hand which kept me safe? I
am not a very religious man but I did believe there was a God
watching over us – but on the other hand it was difficult to
understand His ways when so many men died in their youth and
prime of life.

After a few days I heard that I had been awarded the American
Distinguished Flying Cross for my work in 100 Group. The citation
read:

> Wing Commander Michael Renaut, DFC, for extraordinary
> achievement in aerial flight against the enemy. Serving as a
> Commander of 171 Squadron, Wing Commander Renaut
> distinguished himself by outstanding courage and superior
> aerial skill. Although often attacked by enemy fighters and severe
> anti-aircraft fire, he held his course and led his squadron in the
> successful destruction of numerous enemy targets. His fine
> leadership and devotion to duty were in keeping with the highest
> traditions of the Royal Air Force.

If they'd only known how nearly my 'courage' failed me during
those last months! The Investiture at the US Embassy was a colossal
binge up and your citation was read aloud to all and sundry;

General Bissell pinned my cross on. It was a wonderful 'do', which half my family attended – the Americans, unlike 'Buck House', didn't mind how many friends and relations you brought!!

One amusing incident occurred at the end of February. My mother was passionately fond of jugged hare and she'd asked me if I could get her one before the hare shooting season ended. I got in my car one late afternoon and casually drove round the perimeter track in search of my quarry but I had no luck, even my favourite spot in the bomb dump yielded nothing so I decided, very cautiously, to try outside the aerodrome on the public highway. I knew the risks I was running but I now had a silencer on my rifle and this meant that it made hardly any noise. I eventually spotted a lovely big hare sitting in a field 100 yards from the main road. I stopped the car, got out and looked up and down the road and saw that all was clear so I got back in the car, wound down the passenger's window and took careful aim. Phut! – and the hare fell on its back. I put the rifle on the back seat and was just in the act of getting out when I heard a voice saying: 'And what might you be doing?'

It was one of Lord Leicester's gamekeepers and he said: 'What's your name and where do you come from?'

I had to tell him and was very frightened of the publicity I might have to face!

'Shooting pheasants, are you?' he said.

'Oh no,' I replied, 'the pheasant shooting season's over.'

'Well, what about these two birds?' he said, pointing to a brace of pheasants by a haystack on the other side of the road. I hadn't seen these but neither had he seen my dead hare! 'Let me look in your boot,' he said, so I lifted the lid and showed him it was empty but unfortunately there was a good deal of blood and feathers from previous escapades! 'I have made a note of your rank and name and I shall have to report you for poaching and shooting on the public highway,' he said and I drove off. I spent a very worried afternoon and thought of my good name as a squadron commander and a friend of Lord Leicester and I was frantic. I knew Group Captain Bray after all his warnings wouldn't be very pleased and I knew the police would have me for firing from the public highway. Days passed and nothing happened (I had been back to the field late that night and retrieved my hare with the aid of a torch) and I began to breathe again.

The funny twist to the story was weeks later I asked Lord Leicester if I might shoot some wood pigeons and he agreed readily but said: 'No pheasant mind, you rascal!'

I assured him that I respected the close season and he said: 'Call on my head gamekeeper's cottage and say that you have my permission, otherwise he'll wonder what the bangs in the wood are.'

I accordingly packed my twelve bore, a shovel and decoys in the back of my Hillman and drove round to the gamekeeper's cottage. When I knocked on the door, who should answer but my gamekeeper who had caught me on the main road some weeks earlier. Incredibly he failed to recognise me (I was in sports coat and flannels and not RAF uniform which probably deceived him) so I said that I had permission from Lord Leicester to shoot pigeons in the wood.

'No shooting pheasants, Sir,' he said and I hastily assured him that I wouldn't.

'Ah, I know, Sir,' he said, 'but only a few weeks ago I caught a young RAF officer such as you, poaching pheasants and I had to question him.'

I could hardly keep a straight face and wonder how on earth he'd failed to recognise me!

We used to have great sport at North Creake on the aerodrome shooting hares by the light of headlamps. One used to drive and the other two used to stand up through the sliding roof and fire at hares on the run. It wasn't easy shooting from a moving car but it was grand sport and our best night we bagged fourteen hares.

On 12th May after the war was well and truly over we were permitted to fly our Halifaxes very low over the Ruhr to inspect the damage, for which we'd been, in Bomber Command, responsible. Low flying was the greatest thrill imaginable but you'd got to be quick and precise! I luckily grew out of it in 1942 but not before I'd nearly killed myself! My sister Eileen worked as a secretary at Colthrop Board and Paper Mills near Thatcham, Berkshire and one day I promised her I'd come and 'beat the place up'. They had a look-out post on the roof and on the agreed date at the right time I

arrived ready to show off in my Halifax. I started by zooming over
the roof at 10 feet and pulling up in a steep climb and after repeating
this twice more, I climbed up to 3,000 feet on this sunny day to show
off my Rate 4 (steep) turns! I was executing a brilliant Rate 4 turn to
port and looking down at my sister and her boss, when I stalled and
dived to 400 feet before I regained control! That cured me of the
foolish habit and I never showed off again. (I only had a flight
engineer with me, thank God).

I saw many crashes through low flying and 'beat-ups' – the worst
at Fayid in Egypt when a Hudson with seventeen people on board
beat up the officers' mess, caught the top of the tent at 250 mph and
cartwheeled into the desert. The aeroplane exploded with a terrific
roar and seventeen young men were burnt to death before my eyes
whilst we stood by, utterly helpless in the heat.

I took off with thirteen passengers and sightseers (including
ground staff) and we had a very interesting flight for five hours
looking at the damage and the devastated cities. The damage was
incredible and I took a number of photographs from 150 feet which
came out very well. I shouldn't have cared to live in the Ruhr with
thousand bomber raids and canisters of incendiaries.

The next day one of my Halifax crews was showing off low flying
over the beach at Cromer when it crashed. The pilot was evidently
approaching the beach from seawards and 'beating up' the crowds
on the beaches. On the second run, at high speed, he failed to pull
the aircraft up over the cliffs and flew straight into the cliff face – it
may have been the effect of a strong breeze causing peculiar air
currents. The Halifax exploded and burning pieces showered bathers
on the sands below and eighteen people were killed. I felt most
annoyed as squadron commander that a crew who had survived the
war should kill themselves in this way and I felt most upset at having
to write eight unnecessary letters of sympathy to relatives.

Group Captain Sammy Hoare, who commanded the Mosquito
station at Little Snoring, flew over to North Creake in his Mosquito
as he'd promised to let me fly it. I took over control when we were
airborne and flew along to Cromer to see the wreckage of my
Halifax from the air and later landed the Mosquito. It was a lovely
aeroplane to fly and so light and sensitive after the lumbering
Halifax – I got used to it very easily and wished that I'd flown them

more. Poor Sammy Hoare, who married a WAAF officer from North Creake, was later killed flying a jet in Australia. How senseless it seemed for one of our leading night fighter pilots to be killed in peace-time after surviving six years in Fighter Command.

Yvonne was now expecting our first child any minute and I was more or less at the end of a telephone. She went into a nursing home at York on 10th June and in the early hours of the morning of 11th June I received a phone call from the Matron telling me that I had a son. I had been on a slight thrash the night before in the Mess and I wasn't at all sure in the cold light of day whether I had heard correctly so when I was really awake at about ten o'clock I telephoned the Matron and asked her if it was true. She was most understanding and said that it was perfectly true; I had a son weighing 7½ lbs. and he was to be called Alan. Unfortunately my Rover was in a garage being re-bored so I phoned them and asked if I could take it and they said it was ready. I then drove from North Creake to York at 30 mph all the way because of the running in speed! I have never known a journey take such an age but I was so excited when I saw Yvonne in bed with my son in her arms that I forgot all else in the world.

And so, with the complete and utter disintegration of Nazi Germany, our work came to an end, and although my squadron was not formed until the final phase of the battle, it contributed a small share towards the defeat of our oldest enemies.

On disbandment of my squadron at North Creake I was posted in to No 1 Group in Lincolnshire to command No 103 Squadron at Elsham Wolds. The squadron was equipped with Lancasters which I hadn't yet flown so I had to do a quick conversion course at Lindhome for five days before taking over command. The Lancaster proved to be easy to handle and I soon felt at home in the aeroplane; it was gentle and much more responsive than the Halifax but as I have said before, it wouldn't stand up to so much punishment as the Halifax in battle.

Elsham Wolds (near Brigg and Scunthorpe) proved to be a very pleasant station and was under the command of Group Captain Ronnie Baxter, DFC, and he and I were similar types and hit it off immediately. I liked Group Captain Baxter and he was a most efficient station commander, a great disciplinarian who would stand no nonsense but a man with a great sense of humour. He was the complete opposite to Group Captain Bray, tall, dark haired and handsome with a fine black moustache, unmarried and most eligible! I took up my command on a Friday evening and arrived in the mess in the middle of a party. As I walked in the front door of the officers' mess two officers were being carried out feet first by a cheering crowd of officers and these turned out to be the Dental Officer and the Medical Officer! Both were completely sloshed and I wondered what sort of a unit I had taken over. God help anyone who was taken ill with toothache or tummyache, I thought!

Our squadron's main task at Elsham Wolds was the repatriation of troops from Italy – rather dull work, really, after all the excitement of war, but it was gratifying to see the troops' happiness on landing back in England. Several of them used to lie down and hug the earth they were so pleased to be home! We used to get about twenty troops in the fuselage; it was an uncomfortable trip for them really but we never had any complaints. For some of them it had been four years since they saw England.

It was strange for me in many ways of giving up all my roots in 17 Squadron in Norfolk and getting to know new faces at Elsham Wolds, but I had taken over a famous squadron and it was at least running as an efficient unit. The only person I brought with me was Squadron Leader Robertson for he was a first-class officer and a very likable Scotsman. He took over one of the flights on 103 Squadron. We shared the aerodrome with 100 Squadron commanded by Wing Commander Davis – a squat, cheery Welshman considerably older than I was. With the war over we had considerably more leisure hours and a good deal of our time was spent exploring the local pubs. We held a mess dance and Yvonne came down and spent the night at the hotel in Brigg where she changed into evening dress. We had a wonderful party and drank far too much to be good for us and I remember driving back to the hotel at a very late hour in the morning.

The only 'black' at the party was the sudden disappearance of a padre! Group Captain Baxter and I organised a search and the naughty man was found in bed with a ginger-haired maid from the officers mess! I noticed she was missing during the party and should have put two and two together but I didn't. Baxter was horrified and promptly had the unfortunate man posted elsewhere.

Whenever I wanted to visit Yvonne in Market Weighton I used to borrow Robbie's Morris 8 and drive to the New Holland/Hull ferry and I could be home in an hour and a half. The war over, I was naturally allowed to live out but I only used to spend occasional nights away as I felt that my place was with the squadron. Ronnie Baxter was a bachelor (goodness knows why – and he still is) and consequently he was always on hand. Whenever he went on leave I used to take command of the station (some 1500 men and women) and once he asked me if I would take the church parade on Sunday morning.

Unfortunately I had a thick night on the Saturday night and overslept. I was awoken at five to eight with my adjutant's voice over the telephone saying: 'We're all ready for you, Sir.' I panicked as I was still in pyjamas but hastily pulled on RAF trousers and my greatcoat buttoned up to the neck and rushed out to my car to take the parade at eight a.m. The sight of 1,500 people lined up on the main runway was a somewhat awe-inspiring sight and if they'd know that I had pyjamas on under my greatcoat they would have been very surprised. I felt awfully unshaven but luckily there was no one near enough to notice.

The dentist at Elsham Wolds was a mad keen golfer and asked me if I played; when I said 'No' he said, 'Come on and I'll teach you.' We went across to the little nine hole course near the aerodrome and he started showing me how to play iron shots. We stood alongside the first green and he was clouting balls back towards the clubhouse 160 yards away. He handed me a No 5 iron, teed up a ball for me and suggested I try a shot. I'd never played golf before but had strong hands, wrists and forearms and I hit the ball with all my might. It went like a rocket towards the clubhouse and landed on the corrugated iron roof with a gigantic bang. Members came streaming out to see what was going on and my poor Dental Officer was covered in embarrassment. I can still hit a 5 iron 180 yards but I regret that my handicap is a modest twelve as I can't guarantee direction!

During September I lost one of my best crews in tragic circumstances. I had briefed ten crews to fly to Pomigliano, near Naples, on repatriation but the meteorological report was lousy, with violent electrical storms in the Mediterranean, and I told the crews frankly that I didn't think they'd go. Group however over-ruled me and despite the dangerous weather they decided that our aircraft would go. I told Group HQ that I thought they were crazy and Mediterranean storms were highly dangerous, but my protest counted for nothing and ten Lancasters took off. One aircraft with a full crew and twenty nursing sisters on board (including my gunnery leader, Squadron Leader Whymark, who'd done eighty-five operations over Germany) disintegrated in an electrical storm and crashed in the Mediterranean. When I remonstrated with Group HQ I was politely told that they expected a 1 per cent casualty rate on the job we were doing. I thought and think to this day, that this was a tragic waste of human lives on a task that wasn't vitally urgent.

On 11th October I took off for Berlin with twenty-one crew (including ten army officers) on a sightseeing tour. We landed at Potsdam, just outside Berlin, after 2½ hours in the air and it seemed very strange to us to go across Germany without being shot at! We were billeted at a barrack in Potsdam and were given a lorry to go into Berlin. I was shattered at the damage wrought by Bomber Command and Russian shelling – the whole of the centre of the town was destroyed and in the Potsdamer Platz there wasn't a complete building standing. I took my navigator with me into the Russian sector to have a look at the Chancellery and we spent an hour looking around Hitler's and other offices. I dug about in the rubble and found two or three Iron Crosses, and went to Hitler's bureau drawer and pinched a handful of his personal notepaper! It was most interesting; the whole area was deserted and only guarded by a Russian soldier with a tommy gun who couldn't have been more than fifteen! I couldn't speak any Russian and he didn't know a word of English but we got along well with a sort of sign language. Later we visited the Brandenburg Gate and watched the bartering going on with Russian and Allied soldiers and German civilians. Binoculars, cameras, watches and diamond rings were being traded for cigarettes and chocolate. One of my crew got himself a Leica camera worth £200 for 1,000 Woodbine cigarettes. The first evening we all went to a night club on the outskirts of Berlin and there were six of us at the table ordering the most sumptuous meal and drinking champagne. There was an attractive blonde German singer with the band and we had her over at our table singing songs to our requests – and the whole evening cost ten Players, so we couldn't grumble.

Berlin was in a frightful mess, particularly the outskirts, and there were still hundreds of dead bodies alongside the roads – the stench was frightful but no one seemed to have the will to clean up the mess. There was an underground tube station in the centre of the city which had been hit by a 12,000 lb. bomb and there were over four hundred bodies down there of people who had been sheltering when the bomb fell and penetrated to about 100 feet. This was four months after the end of the war in Europe and yet it had still not been cleared up. There was a sort of lethargy about everyone we met, a sort of forlorn helplessness and people were wandering about the city in a dream. There were no shops in the centre of Berlin – every building was roofless – but there were one or two barter centres open. The principle was that one could buy a pound of coffee in exchange for a pair of Wellington boots size 9! One could buy a pair of size 9 shoes for a dozen eggs. Life was very simple in the city and people were living in shacks built out of the fallen masonry. I didn't find the people antagonistic towards the British but there was undoubtedly a hatred of the Russians – people were kind and helpful, and being able to speak the language was a great help to me. Some of the tube trains were running, even though stations where the dead were still lying where they died, were closed. The visit to Berlin was altogether a sickening experience but it served its purpose in enabling us aircrew to witness the damage caused by concentrated area bombing.

We flew back home after couple of days and practically every member of my crew and the passengers had some piece of loot or another! There were cameras, watches, binoculars, jewellery, fountain pens and even jerry cans of petrol (because of petrol rationing in Britain); we landed at the recognised customs aerodrome in UK – Tibbenham near Cambridge – and I was asked by the customs officer to detail one member of my crew to stay with the Lancaster while a search was made. I picked Flight Lieutenant Blamires, my navigator, with my tongue in my cheek because I knew he had more loot than anyone. A thorough search of the aircraft, undercarriage nacelles, turrets, drawers and cubby holes was made but yielded precisely nothing and when I saw Blamires I asked him how on earth he had managed to get away with it. He pointed out a large panel behind the wireless operator's seat which he had unscrewed and therein had secreted all the loot. Only one member of my crew had declared a Leica camera and had been stung heavily for duty so honesty was not, apparently, the best policy.

On 3rd December 1945 I was posted to Scampton to command No 57 Squadron. Scampton, in Lincolnshire, was only a few miles from Lincoln and was a permanent station. The Station Commander and the Base Commander (an air commodore) both lived out with their wives so there were two lovely RAF houses available on the aerodrome. I immediately got Yvonne up with our new-born son, Alan, and we took up residence in the vast Station Commander's house together with a living-in cook and maid. Yvonne was overawed at the size of the house and the gigantic Aga cooker in the kitchen, but as a squadron commander of some seniority I had a pleasant life and was extremely comfortably housed. No 57 Squadron was equipped with Lincolns, four-engined bombers larger than the Lancaster, but I had virtually lost interest and enthusiasm now with the war over. All we had to do was train, train, train, and formation flying, cross-countries and take offs and landings were the order of the day. When I say that I had lost interest I mean, of course, in the flying; commanding a squadron was still a full-time job and we had to revert to 'dining-in nights' in the Mess and generally returned to peacetime conditions.

It was a glorious life of leisure and Yvonne and I were constantly being invited to the Mess functions or to civilians outside the aerodrome. In January I was invited to join a shoot nearby as a guest of Lord 'X' and there were fourteen guns for some very good partridge drives over the flat Lincolnshire countryside. I remember standing up against a hedge on a main road next to Lord 'X' whilst a crowd of beaters were making their way slowly towards us across a stubble field. There was a cold, high wind blowing and only two partridges got up down wind and unfortunately elected to fly directly over me. Their speed as they approached must have been in the region of Mach 1 and all eyes were upon me. The two partridges came right over my head and I let go both barrels and never touched a feather; Lord 'X' who was standing fifty yards down the road said: 'What happened, Renaut? They looked an easy shot!' I was covered with embarrassment and wished very dearly that he had been at my stand with partridges flying near the speed of sound. I did manage to redeem myself in the afternoon and our bag was 64 brace of partridge, but I still preferred the quiet, unobtrusive use of a rifle and silencer! I had become expert with the rifle even for killing pheasants.

Our squadron mascot was a duck and the poor wretched bird had a liking for beer. Many was the evening when the boys used to stand the duck on the Mess bar counter and put down a saucer of beer, laced with whisky! The sight of the duck, whistled as a coot, falling over on the bar counter brought screams of laughter and seldom have I seen anything funnier! (It didn't seem cruel then as it does now.)

In February we had a visit for lunch from the C-in-C Bomber Command and during the meal he asked me if I had applied for a permanent commission. I said: 'No, Sir. I am being demobbed next month and I'm going back to my old job.' He said he thought I was foolish and that I would be wise to apply for a permanent commission in case civilian life didn't come up to expectations. Knowing that my application would have his blessing I applied for a permanent commission and had a letter back in April awarding me a PC in the rank of substantive flight lieutenant. This unfortunately came too quickly and I hadn't enough time to decide whether I liked civilian life.

I went up to the Air Ministry to see my old friend Air Marshal Tommy Traill and I asked his advice. He told me that as I had only done ten months overseas service it would almost inevitably mean going overseas with no hope of taking Yvonne and Alan, so I reluctantly declined the PC. I often wonder what I should have been doing now had I accepted. The peacetime RAF was a very different thing from wartime and promotion was exceedingly slow – I should probably have been thrown out by now or offered a 'Golden Bowler'.

Just before I left Scampton there was a horrible accident. The aircrew who were mostly unemployed, were put on to cleaning out the flight offices on the first floor of the hangars. A gang of aircrew were busy cleaning the linoleum floor with buckets of petrol and some fool said: 'I know how to dry it out' and before anyone could stop him he struck a match and the whole floor caught fire in a minor explosion. The aircrew were burned to death, overcome by flames and suffocation in seconds. It seemed to me such a senseless tragedy to die like that after having survived an operational tour and I severely reprimanded the fool responsible. He received a severe enough punishment at the subsequent court martial.

I sent Yvonne and Alan home in late February, and on 5th March I received my demobilisation papers at last. This was the moment we'd all been waiting for – the end of the war and back into one's civilian clothes without the discipline of the Services. I certainly had the odd doubts and wondered whether I was doing the right thing, but at that moment life was gay and nothing meant more than going home. But where was home? I had nowhere to live and I had to restart my job in London – where were Yvonne and Alan and I going to live?

First and foremost I had got my gratuity and my pay for three months' leave and I was as free as air. I went to the Demob centre at Wembley Pool and drew my allocation of clothes. Being 6ft. 1½ ins. tall and born with long arms I was disgusted to learn that for a suit I was classified as something between '42" long' and '44" portly'! In other words I couldn't get a suit off the rack; it would have to be specially measured. The shirt, the shoes, the mackintosh, the hat were all straightforward but the suit was a problem. I left with my brown paper parcel (for which I was offered £20 by a spiv outside Wembley Pool) tucked under my arm and hopped a tube to my mother's flat at Redcliffe Square near Earl's Court. I was without a car (I had sold my lovely Rover at an immense profit), without a home, without my RAF life and I felt very alone there in London, but certainly not unhappy.

I caught a train from King's Cross and got back to my wife's home in Market Weighton with her mother and two aunts and there I spent a glorious three months' leave and rest. I opened certain appeal campaigns for the RAF and gave a number of lectures to ATC cadets and Royal Observer Corps units in Yorkshire and life was full and very pleasant.

The Royal Observer Corps did a marvellous job in the war and they got very little credit for it either in histories of the war or in autobiographies like mine, but let me say here and now that the ROC were a magnificent organisation made up of volunteers from all walks of life who spent their time in the open air plotting aircraft movements, reporting and pinpointing crashes and generally making themselves indispensible to the RAF . . . they did a fine job and often in the worst possible weather conditions without ever complaining.

Epilogue

On 1st June I started my job again at J. Lyons & Co Ltd, at their headquarters, Cadby Hall, and I was appointed as Manager of the Swiss Roll factory with one hundred and twenty staff and an annual turnover of over a million pounds. Lyons were an extremely nice firm to work for but they had no time for inefficiency. Even then, after the war, a certain fear crept into my life. Would I be good enough to hold down the job? Did I know enough about bakery? Was I capable of controlling a mainly female civilian staff? Could I forget the past and not talk about the war? People had stayed at Cadby Hall throughout the war producing food – a reserved occupation; how would they react to a retired bomber pilot?

All these questions had to be answered but it took time, and settling down I found *most* difficult. Luckily there was a handful of us ex-servicemen, Douglas Fisher, Jack Brandon, Bill Hare, Percy Evans, Arthur Ritchie – they all came back to Lyons as I did, and are all still there happily settled in again.

I stuck it and my little third floor flat in London's Buckingham Palace Road, but as time wore on I felt most unsettled and I missed the comparative freedom of the Services. My hours were 7 a.m. to 5 p.m. in a hot and busy factory for £15 per week and I hadn't really got the confidence in my own ability to stay. In 1949 I was promoted and was appointed Manager of the French Pastry factory – a complex and busy factory and the most difficult of the bakeries to run. I had a wonderful factory foreman, Joe Webb, but I was still unsure of my ability at twenty-six to run the place efficiently. After all, I had left Lyons at nineteen to join the RAF and all I could do well was fly an aeroplane! What good was this qualification to them? I had to prove myself and it took me four years with that wonderful company to do it. Nevertheless a lot of the work was beyond me; I simply hadn't got the experience and how could I have at twenty-six? In a way I still feared the sack and yet I'd burned my boats in the RAF by refusing a permanent commission and where could I turn to? Thousands of ex-servicemen must have gone through what I did and resettlement in peace-time was no easy matter.

I was so fed up with living in a small flat in London with no garden for my children that after four years with J. Lyons & Co Ltd Yvonne and I discussed the question of leaving them, but who did we know to offer us a job? We racked our brains until Yvonne said: 'What about Mr Tharby?' He ran a motor and engineering business in Datchet near Windsor, and was an old friend of my parents. He is an extraordinary man; self-made, ruthless in business, somewhat of a poseur with his white silk shirt and white silk tie and a large Stetson hat always wanting to look like a Texan! He'd got where he'd got, a wealthy man, on his own ability but he was as tough as nails and a hard nut to crack. Several people warned me against working for Tharby but I liked him and admired him for building up such a good business and I was prepared to chance it, so we wrote him a letter in 1949 asking for an interview. He lived in a gorgeous house in Bournemouth and invited me down. We had a long discussion in an informal atmosphere and in the end he offered me General Managership of his Motor Business and engineering factory. I didn't know anything about either except that I'd played about with my own two cars and sold one at a colossal profit, but I agreed to start on 1st May 1950.

I left Lyons, having put my case to my director, Geoffrey Salmon and his deputy, Brian Salmon, and they were both very sympathetic, found a small house in Datchet, and started with Tharby on 1st May. For the first few months I felt completely out of my depth but I applied myself to learning about motor cars and engineering drawings with as much help as I could get from the fifty staff. It wasn't an easy job learning the motor business, which contains a number of thieves and rogues in the secondhand car side, but I had to get down to it and in two years I was running the place reasonably efficiently. I feared the sack daily as Tharby was a hard taskmaster and expected quick results from me, which I wasn't really able to give, but I was learning and, so far, had given him reasonable satisfaction. A self-made man is usually impatient at inefficiency and usually reckons he can do the job better than anyone else (probably quite rightly) but I weathered the early years without being sacked and although I made some bad mistakes I was managing to hold the job down – and increased the turnover eightfold in as many years. My chief was a perfectionist and nothing less than perfection was going to suit him.

The years wore on and in 1957 when I was aged thirty-seven he made me a director and gave me a 25 per cent share holding. This was progress with Tharby. He didn't trust anyone but even went on a luxury cruise that year to Australia and left the business in my care for three months! This was progress for me . . . in thirty years no one had signed Tharby's cheques for him nor run his business for him alone and unaided.

Things continued very amicably until August 25th 1961 when I suddenly without warning had a nervous breakdown. (There is no such thing in medical parlance; it is referred to as a 'nervous depression'.) I felt ghastly for six long months through a hard and soul-destroying winter – and despite Yvonne's help and my kind doctor's help the depression continued for six weary months and I felt more ghastly and depressed each day until I could no longer face my friends and relations. My life was a misery – an unrewarding, painful misery relieved by nothing. I drank a little, we entertained a little but nothing would pull me round and how Yvonne stuck my mental state for six long months I shall never know. Tharby was now getting impatient and his ruthlessness came to the fore – I made feeble excuses and he blamed the winter slump in the Motor Industry and said I must bloody well pull myself together. I couldn't expect sympathy and I naturally didn't get any – he was my chief and he was watching me go downhill.

Thanks to John Gallimore, my doctor and Yvonne, I eventually, but albeit reluctantly, agreed to see a psychiatrist – a brilliant London man – at the end of January 1962 and he immediately put his finger on the trouble . . . the war! I could not bring myself to believe that seventeen years after the war I should be affected mentally but now there is absolutely no doubt about it. I used to have nightmares of being abandoned in a burning Halifax high over a target and used to wake up shouting and screaming – I don't get those nightmares any more now after fourteen weeks in a nursing home. I was cured by drugs and the very able handling of my case by this eminent and competent neurologist and by his assistant, Doctor B. Here was a young man, thirty years of age, who could read me like an open book. He steered me through the most anxious fourteen weeks of my life and my present well-being I owe almost entirely to these kind and skilful men and to my Yvonne, who stuck by me nobly.

Seventeen years after the war my fears brought me down to the worst mental depression possible but now that I am cured I have no more fears in life. I am ready to make a fresh start with confidence that I never had before. I am told that to have bottled up my fears for six years during the prime of my youth had pulled me down. Those long penetrations into Germany, the unutterable strain of facing searchlights and flak and deadly night fighters took its toll of my health at long last, but now I can look back on my fears and laugh at them. Need I have been so frightened in the war? – why should I have been so petrified over the target? It was fear based on the unknown, fear of losing one's precious life. Fear takes many forms, fear based on ignorance and imagination. I believe that those who claim they were never frightened are either liars or completely without imagination. Only a comparative few of Bomber Aircrew lost their nerve during the war, and hard as it may seem now, they had to pay the penalty of fear by public ignominy. But fear could spread through a squadron like wildfire and unless the rot was stopped quickly and at source – there was no telling how it could have spread.

There must have been a weakness in my make-up. Who was I but a humble bomber pilot – a nobody? Fear took its toll of me but there are thousands today who faced the horrors and dangers that I faced and they are normal, sensible citizens. Undoubtedly they had their fears as I did but they never weakened – people like Cheshire, Tait, Iveson, Young, Bill Kofoed, Nigel Bennett – they had great strength of character and were all extremely brave men. Terribly brave – Cheshire did over a hundred operations over Germany and German-occupied territory but his nerve remained strong. His turn to religion after the war may have been a result of the fears and horror of war but to look at him one would say: 'Here is a brave man who faced sudden death for six years and never faltered.' Group Captain Young, whom I knew so well, now lives in Leighton

Buzzard with his fine family. He survived, however, and his strong religious faith probably brought him through the war. I weakened, but these brave men continue to go through life unaffected.

War is now unthinkable but undoubtedly, were it to come, brave men would again offer their services in battle as they did in 1939/1945 – it is to these men – Englishmen and fearless, that this book of mine is dedicated.

Index

Aasen Fjord (Trondheim) 71, 72, 80, 81
Aberystwyth 18
Accra 120, 122, 125
Acton 15
Addison, Air Vice-Marshal E.B. 146
Alexandria 114
Almazo 116
Ames, Flying Officer L.E.G. 19
Ammon, Flight Lieutenant Fred 133
Angiers, Wing Commander 18
Aqir 98, 100, 102, 109

Babbacombe 16, 17, 18
Bates, Flying Officer 153, 164
Battle of Britain 30, 85
Baxter, Group Captain Ronnie, 172, 173, 174
Beardmore, Sergeant 39, 40
Bell, Sergeant 51
Bennett, Air Vice-Marshal D.C.T. 41, 72, 87
Bennett, Isabel 117, 143
Bennett, Rosemary 117
Bennett, Wing Commander Nigel 117, 118, 142, 143, 183
Bevington, Wing Commander 142, 146, 149

Bickerdike 107, 108, 144
Bircham Newton 142
Bishop, Mr. 118
Bissell, General 169
Bitter Lake 106
Blamires, Flight Lieutenant 176, 177
Brandon, Jack 181
Bray, Group Captain N.A.N. 146, 149, 150, 151, 155, 169, 173
Bremen 86, 90, 91, 92, 99, 163
Brest 50, 51, 53, 64, 110
Bridlington 70
Bryan, Flight Lieutenant 107
Butler, Flight Lieutenant 160

Cairo 99, 112, 114, 116, 118
Calder, Pilot Officer Jock (later Wing Commander) 36, 44, 143
Cambridge (Marshalls Flying School) 19, 22, 23, 24
Carr, Air Vice-Marshal Roddy 139, 141, 148
Carr, Phyl 143
Cheshire, Geoffrey (later Group Captain,) 45, 66, 83, 87, 127, 129, 143, 184

Cheshire, Group Captain Leonard 45
Chisholm, Senior Air Staff Officer Rory 155
Churchill 106, 168
Clack, Squadron Leader 144
Clayton, Squadron Leader, 143
Cobham, Sir Alan 15
Coke, Elizabeth 149
Coke, Thomas 149
Collins, Pilot Officer Tim 57, 65, 72, 73, 75, 76, 81, 83, 84, 86, 87, 89, 90, 91, 98, 99, 102, 108, 112, 115, 124, 162
Cologne 43, 66, 85, 86, 88, 110
Combe, Lady Sylvia 149, 150, 151, 164
Combe, Simon 150
Corbisier 32
Cottesmore 50
Coventry 26, 27
Critchley, Air Commodore 18
Croft 57
Croft, Jack 108, 109
Cromer 171
Croydon 15

Dambuster Squadron 88
Darlington 36, 37, 43, 49, 62, 63, 82
Datchet 182
Davis, Wing Commander 173
Derry, John 117, 118
Docking 77, 78
Driffield (No 2 Blind Approach Training Course) 56
Duisberg 75
Dunkerque 44, 45, 48, 49, 53

Dunkirk 84
Dunning White, Wing Commander 155
Düsseldorf 44, 45, 61

El Alamein 98, 106, 111
Elsham Wolds 172, 173, 174
Ennis, Flying Officer 56
Espley 32
Essen 54, 70, 75, 76, 77, 86, 87, 88, 89, 110, 141, 164
Evans, Percy 181

Fair 32
Farnborough 117, 118
Fayid 103, 104, 107, 108, 114, 116, 171
Feasy, Sergeant 158
Field, Trevor 134
Fisher, Douglas 181
Frandsen 43, 44
Frankfurt 37, 39, 49, 109, 162
Freetown 123, 125

Gallimore, John 183
Garrison, Colonel 104
Gaskell, Squadron Leader 146
'GEE' 42
Gibson, Wing Commander Guy 88
Glasgow 32

Haliopolis 112
Hamburg 74, 83
Handley-Page, Sir Frederick 60
Hanover 42, 43
Hare, Bill 181
Hartley, Flight Lieutenant Sam

135, 139
Harvey, Lady Mary 149, 150, 164
Harris, Air Marshal Sir Arthur, 56, 84, 86, 90, 143
Heraklion (Crete) 61, 106, 107, 108, 109
Herbert 32
Herne Bay 15, 26
Hoare, Group Captain Sammy 171, 172
Hoskinson, Air Commodore 75, 78
Howard, Arthur 114
Howard, Leslie 113-114
Hull 53
'H2S' 42

IFF (Identification Friend or Foe) 49, 121
Iles, Wing Commander Gordon 135, 136
Iveson, Hank 61, 74, 107, 108, 110, 127, 132, 144, 184

James, Flying Officer 158
Jarman, Wing Commander 'Bull' 37
Jerusalem 116

Kabrit 98
Kent, Duke of 64, 139
Kiel 39, 40, 41, 58, 60, 99, 110, 164, 165, 167
Kinloss (No 19 Operational Training Unit) 32, 34, 35, 71
Kirkpatrick, Pilot Officer 45, 48, 49

Kitson, Family 152
Kofoed, Bill 81, 139, 143, 184
Kornegay, Lieutenant 139

Lashbrook, Squadron Leader, 94
Lavery, Hugh 80
Lawrence, W.J. 93
Leconfield (No 28 Halifax Conversion Course) 59
Lee, Dicky 30
Leicester, Countess of 147
Leicester, Earl of 147, 149, 150, 164, 168, 169, 170
Leicester, Elizabeth & Tom 150
Lister 67
Lossiemouth 74
Lowry, Pilot Officer 37, 38, 39, 41

McDonald, Flight Sergeant 158
Macleod, Jock 24, 32
Magdeburg 55
Malet-Warden, Sergeant 40
Mallorie, Pilot Officer 19, 20, 23, 24
Mannheim 65, 67
Marston Moor 127, 129
Mehta, Dr & Mrs 125, 126
Mercer, Squadron Leader Jock 37, 49, 53, 58, 62, 65, 66
Mersa Matruh 104
Meynell, Lawrence 95
Middleton St George 36, 37, 39, 40, 58, 62, 74, 78, 81, 82, 88, 98
Montgomery, General 106
Moosejaw 24, 25

Morris, Sergeant 66
München-Gladbach 87

Neal, Bob 143
Newborn, Sergeant Don 49, 50
Newton Abbot 17
Norman, Wing Commander Bob 127
North Creake 76, 146, 150, 151, 152, 154, 155, 157, 160, 161, 170, 172
Nuremburg 55

Oakes, Richard 19, 21, 23, 25, 26, 27, 28, 29, 32, 139
O'Leary, Colonel Patrick (Colonel Guerrisse & 'Monsieur Courage') 94
Orfordness 49, 50
Ostend 50, 53
Ostree, Commandant 144
Owen, Flight Lieutenant 59

Palestine 98
Peenemünde 56
Pershke, John 21, 31, 32
Petts-Frazer, Ralph 19
PFF (Pathfinder Force) 41, 87
Pocklington 137, 138
Pomigliano 174
Price, Wing Commander Seymour 97

RAF Volunteer Reserve
Rawson, Cynthia 19
Raymond, Geoff 115
Reculver 15
Renaut, Alan 162, 172, 178, 179

Renaut, Eileen 170
Renaut, Yvonne (nee Campbell) 117, 131, 133, 134, 139, 140, 141, 152, 153, 159, 161, 162, 164, 172, 173, 174, 177, 178, 179, 182, 193
Richardson, Flight Lieutenant 24
Richardson, Squadron Leader 135
Riches, Squadron Leader 148
Robertson, Squadron Leader 148, 151, 173
Rolfe, Squadron Leader 128
Royal Air Force:
No 1 Group 172
No 4 Group (Bomber) 127, 144, 147, 148
No 100 Group 146, 147, 148, 162, 167, 168, 173
10 Squadron 97
57 Squadron 177
76 Squadron 36, 37, 60, 144
78 Squadron 37, 57 71, 85, 144
103 Squadron 172, 173
171 Squadron 146, 147, 155, 168, 173
199 Squadron 146, 147
214 Squadron 146
617 Squadron 36
Babbacombe 1st Receiving Wing 16, 17, 18
No 2 Middle East Training School 109
No 8 Pathfinder Bomber Group
No 22 Personnel Transit